D1360487

CREATIVE CHICAGO

CREATIVE CHICAGO

From *The Chap-Book*
to the University

HENRY REGNERY

Introduction by Joseph Epstein

CHICAGO HISTORICAL

BOOKWORKS

1993

PUBLISHED BY
CHICAGO HISTORICAL BOOKWORKS
831 MAIN STREET
EVANSTON, ILLINOIS 60602

DESIGN BY CAMERON POULTER

ILLUSTRATIONS BY SCOTT HOLLINGUE

PRINTED IN THE UNITED STATES OF AMERICA

Library of Congress Cataloging-in-Publication Data
Regnery, Henry, 1912–
Creative Chicago : from the chap-book to the
University / Henry Regnery ;
introduction by Joseph Epstein.
p.   cm.
includes index.
ISBN 0-924772-24-7
1. Chicago (Ill.)—intellectual life.
2. American literature—
Illinois—Chicago—history and criticism.
3. Chicago (Ill.) in literature. i. title.
F548.3.R44 1993
977.3'11—DC20   93-11130
CIP

10 8 6 4 2 1 3 5 7 9

Acknowledgements

THE PAPERS WHICH make up the following book were written over a period of years, and for different occasions: two for the Chicago Literary Club and two others for publication in the quarterly *Modern Age*. The Chicago Literary Club has been holding its "Exercises," as they are called, every Monday evening during the winter months since 1884 when a member reads a paper. The paper which begins the present book is on the subject of early Chicago publishing and had the prophetic title "Against the Stream." Another Literary Club paper was devoted to the history of the literary magazine founded in Chicago in 1880, *The Dial*.

Two papers included in the book were originally published in the quarterly *Modern Age* and were written at the suggestion of the editor, George A. Panichas: one on the autobiography of Louis Sullivan and the other on the biography of Robert M. Hutchins by Harry S. Ashmore. It was with George Panichas' advice and encouragement that these various papers were gathered together into the present book.

For permission to quote from the Dreiser biography by W. A. Swanberg I wish to thank McIntosh & Otis, Inc., as agents for the author, and to thank Harry S. Ashmore for permission to quote from his book *Unseasonable Truths: The Life of Robert M. Hutchins*, and John Pilkington, Jr. for permission to quote from his book, *Henry Blake Fuller*. I also wish to thank Scott Hollingue for his striking illustrations used throughout the book.

Finally for the form of the book I am indebted to my old Chicago friend Carl Guldager. It was he who organized the papers written for different occasions over a period of years and edited them into a coherent book.

Henry Regnery

Contents

Introduction
by Joseph Epstein

H ENRY REGNERY, THE author of these impressively informative and economically composed essays on Chicago writers, publishers, editors, the University of Chicago's President Robert Hutchins, and the architect Louis Sullivan, is a cultivated man hungry for culture. More specifically, he is hungry for culture in Chicago, the city where he was born and has lived much the greatest part of his life. Although neither a dark nor despairing writer, Henry Regnery's essays in this book can scarcely be read without sensing the feeling of sadness behind them that the great train of culture—of culture understood as one of the profound dreams of human aspiration—seemed once to be heading for his native city but had, somehow, been badly derailed en route and may never stop here again.

Henry Regnery has been nicely positioned, both by chronology and by geography, to write this book. As he recounts in the first chapter of his *Memoirs of A Dissident Publisher*, he was born in 1912, in the Chicago suburb of Hinsdale, to a family whose head, his father, was a successful manufacturer of textiles. Regnery's lineage is German on his father's side, English and Welsh on his mother's. But more important is his psychological and spiritual lineage, which is small town, hard-working, upstanding, self-sufficient. Growing up in Hinsdale, Regnery, now in his early eighties, remembers that the town had two blacksmiths and a harness maker and that most deliveries were made by horse-drawn wagons. Henry Regnery is himself a link between the old and the new middlewestern worlds of which he writes in *Creative Chicago*.

"The twelve years I attended public school," Regnery writes, "almost exactly covered the period between the end of World War I and the beginning of the Great Depression. During those years Hinsdale changed from a rather simple, unassuming small town to an aggressive, self-assertive [and today, one might add, quite wealthy] suburb—a process that typifies what was happening in the country as a whole. It was the time during which the transition from the nineteenth to the twentieth century was completed."

Having been born when and where he was gives Henry Regnery a helpful perspective on culture—and particularly on literary culture—in Chicago. Having been born the son of the man who was his father, too, gives him an interesting angle on his subject. When Henry Regnery informed his successful businessman father that he intended to devote his days to publishing, his father, he reports in the afterword to this book, remarked: "Well, if you ever start making money, you'll probably be publishing the wrong sort of books." There are, I suppose, a number of ways of interpreting that response, but I believe that the most sound interpretation is that Regnery's father knew that success in business and success in culture were not at all the same thing. The remark bespeaks a man of character and insight.

The question lurking behind so many of the essays in *Creative Chicago* is: Why has literary culture—with culture now understood as a network of institutions and relationships surrounding the creation of literature—not taken permanent hold in Chicago? One could perhaps answer the question quickly by laying the blame on middlewestern philistinism, but this, as Henry Regnery realizes, will not do. In refutation of so easy an answer, one need only mention that Chicago has had throughout this century a flourishing musical culture and remains a center where young musicians are not only provided with the means to develop their art but the institutions through which to earn their livings in the performance of that art. The same, alas, is not true for literature.

What makes this situation all the more anomalous is that the middlewest, of which Chicago has traditionally been spiritually the capital city, has long been fruitful in the production of writers. Ronald Weber, a professor of American Studies at Notre Dame, has recently produced a book with the title *The Midwestern Ascendancy in American Writing*. Professor Weber dates this ascendancy from just after the close of the Civil War to the beginning of the career of Hart Crane. The cavalcade of names of writers he trots out who were born or came to maturity in the middlewest is not unimpressive: it includes Hamlin Garland, James Whitcomb Riley,

Booth Tarkington, Theodore Dreiser, Henry B. Fuller, Floyd Dell, Edgar Lee Masters, Vachel Lindsay, Zona Gale, Sherwood Anderson, Ring Lardner, Willa Cather, Sinclair Lewis, F. Scott Fitzgerald, Ernest Hemingway, and Glenway Westcott. Pushing up the chronology of Professor Weber's study slightly, one can add the names of James T. Farrell, Richard Wright, and Saul Bellow.

The ascendancy itself might be said to begin both chronologically and symbolically with William Dean Howells, who was born and grew up in Columbus, Ohio. It begins chronologically with Howells because he was the first of the middlewestern writers to achieve a significantly national reputation; and it begins symbolically with him, I believe, because he was also among the first of the middlewestern writers to feel the need to leave the middlewest for the east, which Howells did in 1860, when he travelled to Boston to meet James Russell Lowell, Oliver Wendell Holmes, Sr. and the publisher James T. Fields for lunch at the Tremont Hotel. "Well James," said Holmes to Lowell at this lunch, "this is something like the apostolic succession; this is the laying on of hands." Howells was in time to succeed Lowell as editor of *The Atlantic Monthly*, and when he left his job as editor of *The Atlantic Monthly* to take up the job of editor of *Harper's* in 1885, it was said that, with his departure, the center of American literary culture had shifted from Boston to New York.

That center of American literary culture was never truly in Chicago, even though for a time it looked as if the city might become such a center. In *Makers and Finders*, his five-volume literary history of the United States, Van Wyck Brooks devoted a chapter of his *The Confident Years, 1895–1915* to "Chicago: 1910." In this chapter he wrote:

> With every year the Middle West assumed a larger and larger role
> in the literary life of the country. Novelists, poets and story-tellers,
> emerging there on every hand, had been followed by leaders in crit-
> icism and leaders in thought like Veblen, Irving Babbitt and Paul
> Elmer More, and Chicago seemed on the point of becoming what
> H. L. Mencken was to call it soon, the literary capital of the United
> States. There Dreiser had begun to write, with George Ade and

"Mr. Dooley," there Robert Herrick flourished, with Garland and Fuller, and Ring Lardner and Sherwood Anderson were already at work in the city that Hemingway and John Dos Passos knew as boys. Vachel Lindsay, Masters and Sandburg, the poets, were appearing. Observing Chicago a few years later, Mencken said that for a score of years almost every literary movement of importance in the country had originated under the shadow of the stockyards. Nine times out of ten the writers with "something peculiarly American to say" had some connection with Chicago, Mencken remarked, for either they had been born there or they had got their start there or passed through there in the days they were young and tender.

Floyd Dell, in *Homecoming*, his autobiography, confirms this and gives a good eyewitness account of those days in Chicago from the perspective of a young man serving his novitiate as a writer. Dell was from Davenport, Iowa, and, like many an aspiring middlewestern writer, made Chicago the first leg on what he hoped would be a journey to literary fame. He worked in Chicago as an assistant editor on *The Friday Literary Review*. He was among those young men and women who often met at A. C. McClurg's Bookstore, where they would come to sell their review copies and stay to discuss the great writers of the past and argue about who among their contemporaries had a chance to achieve greatness in the future. Dell saw in this Chicago group "a growing youthful body of American literary taste, which had nourished itself upon the very best European literature and had civilized modern standards." But this group, too, Floyd Dell himself among them, would gradually depart Chicago.

The world Floyd Dell describes in *Homecoming* is that quasi-bohemian of newspapermen with literary ambitions that was most characteristic of literary culture in the first two decades of this century. This was a time when newspapers were often the training ground for young writers—their university, in effect, for many American writers were not college-educated—and Chicago, a town with many papers and a colorful journalistic tradition, provided young writers with work. A great editor such as Henry Justin Smith, of *The Daily News*, went out of his way to hire writers and used to instruct his reporters to read Balzac in order to master their craft. Perhaps the best account of this world is to be found in the pages of Ben Hecht's autobiography, *A Child of the Century*, which is filled with amusing anecdotage about the carryings-on of the Chicago literati of the first decade of the century. Among the most famous of these anecdotes is the one about Hecht and the poet Maxwell Bodenheim charging admission at the Dill Pickle Club to debate the question of whether people who came to hear such debates were or were not fools. Hecht claimed they were, Bodenheim agreed, and they took the money and departed the stage. About these years, which were later described as the so-called Chicago literary renaissance, Hecht said that a lot more talking and drinking than writing got done.

Although he might be amused by such antics, Henry Regnery does not pine for the return of such gaudy—and not very rich— literary culture. He has, my sense is, something very different in mind. In 1990, Regnery wrote a slender volume, a brief history, on the Cliff Dwellers, a Chicago club founded by the novelist Hamlin Garland atop Orchestra Hall on Michigan Boulevard. After a middlewestern upbringing, Garland had worked in Boston, then returned to the middlewest to settle in Chicago, in 1892, a time when the city, as he would later put it, "from having been a huge, muddy market-place, was about to take its place as one of the literary capitals of the world." After many years in Chicago, Garland determined to form a club where workers in all the arts might meet to talk about those things in which they were most passionately interested. In a letter of 1907 describing his plans for such a club, Garland wrote:

> Broadly speaking, this club will bring together men of artistic and literary tastes who are now widely scattered among the various social and business organizations of Chicago and unite them with artists, writers, architects and musicians of the city in a club whose purposes are distinctly and primarily aesthetic, taking hints from the Players, The National Arts and the Century Association of New York. The membership is to be composed of, first—

art[ists],—that is to say, painters, sculptors, novelists, poets, musicians, architects, historians, illustrators, and those who make handicraft and art. Second—distinguished men in other professions who are patrons of art, or sympathetic with the fundamental purpose of the club.

When the novelist Robert Herrick, who was a founding member and who also taught at the University of Chicago, addressed the Cliff Dwellers, he expressed sentiments, there can be little doubt, that the author of *Creative Chicago* would entirely endorse. Herrick noted:

> I take it . . . that the opening of this club has very real significance for the community of Chicago. It means that those of us who are engaged in the practise of the arts, who are interested in the expression of our national life in something other than material accomplishments and mere efficiency, are to have a home, a gathering place where, in true fellowship, with sympathy and understanding and mutual helpfulness, we may meet together, and help create that life of the arts which will make future creation of real worth and significance more possible, if not for ourselves, for those others who are to come after and take up our work.

During its best years, the Cliff Dwellers not only provided a meeting place for the like-minded among workers in the arts in Chicago but also provided a place for the cross-pollinization of ideas and discussion with similar people from elsewhere. The minutes of the Cliff Dwellers Club, Henry Regnery notes in his book, included the following names as visitors: Vachel Lindsay, Ferdinand Leger, Arnold Bennett, John Galsworthy, George Santayana, Theodore Dreiser, Igor Stravinsky, William Butler Yeats, and Lady Gregory and the Irish Players. Not an unimpressive roster.

The Cliff Dwellers still exists, but, so far as artistic and literary culture are concerned, in greatly attenuated form. The Tavern Club in Chicago, another dining club founded by people in the arts, presumably to meet to talk about their work, is today chiefly dominated, in its membership, by businessmen and lawyers. The Arts

Club, another such Chicago institution, seems more and more a women's lunch club with gallery showings of visual art and occasional poetry readings and lectures, than a place for artists to meet. None of these in any case faintly resemble the Cliff Dwellers in its glory days, a place where serious people met to talk about serious things. What is more, it seems unlikely that an institution such as the Cliff Dwellers is ever likely to be revivified—at any rate, not in Chicago.

Not that this draining of literary and artistic culture from Chicago is an altogether recent phenomenon. When *The New Yorker* writer A. J. Liebling first came to Chicago in 1938, having heard about the literary revolution that had gone on here years before, he found the city a distinct disappointment, which he recorded several years later in his book *Chicago: The Second City*. "For a city where, I am credibly informed, you couldn't throw an egg in 1925 without braining a great poet," Liebling wrote, "Chicago is hard up for writers." When he returned to Chicago in the late 1940s and early '50s, wherever Liebling and his wife would go in Chicago he would run into Nelson Algren, who seemed to stand for all that was most characteristic in literature in Chicago. "A man named Milton Mayer was another standard act," Liebling wrote. "The rest of the party was usually made up of admiring patrons of the arts and the members of the faculty of the University of Chicago."

Things did not improve with time. In the magazine *Furioso*, W. B. Scott, a teacher of drama at Northwestern University, wrote "Chicago Letter," a parody of the old pretentious literary letter that used to appear in little magazines, during the height of the vogue for existentialism, in which the very idea of literary culture in Chicago was made to appear ridiculous. "Agony, a sense of plight," Scott's parody portentously begins, "a sense of agony, plight—such, one soon perceives, are the attributes of the Chicago of our time." In one of his most hilarious paragraphs, Scott writes:

> Other facts suggest the city's agony. A fortnight after my arrival
> I read in the *Cicero Quarterly* (which last week ceased publication)
> of the dissolution of the Goose Island Sartre Club, whose president, with ironic ambivalence, rather than commit suicide had

taken a job as a check-out boy in a supermarket. Early today, as I started to compose this letter, Jeremy Irk phoned to tell me that the Rogers Park *Cercle Rimbaud* is down to nine members, eight of whom do not speak to each other. Yet with all this endemic apathy, one learns of eruptions of violence as well. . . . In the dim alleys of the South Side, I am told, "goon squads from the Aristotle A.C. sally out after nightfall to sack hostile bookshops or worse. Such things are, to be sure, a kind of action, although I cannot say what hope one is to take from it.

At the same time that the institutional life necessary to culture has all but disappeared in Chicago—*Poetry* magazine, about which Henry Regnery writes in this book, is still very much a going concern, and a few trade publishers struggle on—Chicago continues somehow to be a city that is, if not particularly good to writers, then somehow good for writing. Why so many good writers have been born or have spent ample periods of time here is a question never satisfactorily answered. It may be that there is something intrinsic to Chicago, which some have called the last great American city, that keeps writers on the main job. Chicago is not, like New York, a world city, where the mechanics of publicity grind away and where writers can indulge the deception that they are crucial to quotidian life; nor, like Los Angeles or Houston, a ghastly freeway city of the future; nor, again, like San Francisco, a perhaps too pretty city, the equivalent of Bloomingdale's Department Store, except out of doors and with hills. It may be, too, that there is something about Chicago, with its business spirit and penchant for corruption, with its general neglect of writers, that is healthy for writers, reminding them that there is a larger and more pressing reality in the world than that represented by the publisher's lunch or the poetry reading or the book-signing.

If Chicago does continue to produce writers, these writers, then as now, do not often remain in Chicago. Not so long ago one sign of a writer's success was that he was able to take himself to New York, where, clearly, the literary action was. A success in Chicago seemed to connote a bush-league success at best. For writers of my own generation and the generation before mine, the feeling used to be

that, at some point, one had to take on New York, or more specifically Manhattan. New York was where literary reputations were
made; New York was where all the important magazines and publishers and agents were. In New York, meeting regularly with fellow
writers, lunching with publishers, doing frequent business with
editors, plotting with one's agent, one can come to believe that
writing is at the center of the world's literary business and, by
extension, one can come to believe in one's own importance.

Young writers no longer feel this way about New York. For them
New York is not a city they feel they must conquer; they scarcely
feel they have to visit it. This doesn't mean that they are content to
remain in Chicago, if they were born here or were middlewesterners
who briefly settled here. Where once New York was indisputably
the center of literary culture in this country, it is now so chiefly in
the institutional sense: the publishers, slick magazines, agents, and
engines of publicity remain in New York. But, increasingly, writers
are finding jobs in universities—and in universities all over the
country. As the audience for serious books seems less and less
dependable, as what even constitutes a serious book is no longer
quite so clear, as publishers are less willing to bring along literary
talent at a gradual pace, fewer and fewer young men and women
with literary aspirations are willing to risk the market. Instead they
take, where they can get them, jobs in universities, chiefly teaching
writing. This has its own sad effects. It takes writers out of the world
and hence out of the realm of non-academic experience. It is also
literarily incestuous in that students tend to follow too closely their
teachers—and writing was, until relatively recently never taught,
but instead, by each writer going at things in his own way,
learned—so that much contemporary writing has begun to have an
all too similar, even assembly-line look.

Henry Regnery is too realistic genuinely to hope for a revival of
literary culture in Chicago of the kind Hamlin Garland sought. My
sense is that he does not in the least expect something resembling the
eighteenth-century coffee-house culture of Samuel Johnson, Oliver
Goldsmith, and Edward Gibbon to show up in Chicago; nor anything like the twice monthly dinners attended in Paris in the nineteenth century at the Restaurant Magny by Flaubert, the brothers

Goncourt, and Sainte-Beuve; nor even to recapture something of what the young F. Scott Fitzgerald felt when, at the time he first came to live in Manhattan, from his cab he spotted his Princeton classmate Edmund Wilson on the street and thought of him representing what he termed "the Metropolitan Spirit."

All this represents a true but nonetheless idealized past. The un-idealized present was perhaps most accurately represented at a Chicago literary conference of nearly ten years ago, where a young writer named James Park Sloan, who has himself been trained at the University of Iowa Writers' Workshop, allowed that it was his sense that such community as exists among young Chicago writers is to be found in college writing programs in the area; and where another young man on the same panel chipped in by saying that his own days at the University of Iowa represented "the first and last literary community I have ever been in."

Nor is Henry Regnery likely for a moment to believe that the network of institutions necessary to a full literary life—publishers, magazines, book reviews, agents, and the rest—has any chance to re-emerge in Chicago. Viewing the contemporary Chicago literary scene, he is likely to make out no more than the hodge-podge of university presses, a few brave independent publishers, no magazines of true distinction (with the exception of *Poetry*, which continues to have standing in the greater world), no consistently serious book reviews, a handful of struggling agents, and, as always, innumerable writers struggling to work out their own visions. The editor of *Another Chicago Magazine*, an appropriately named and now defunct journal, was probably correct when he said that Chicago doubtless continues to have a general "influence on individual writers. But there is no school, no genre, and the city doesn't necessarily have a unity influence on its writers anymore." This seems, somehow, sad.

I remarked at the outset that Henry Regnery was neither a dark nor a despairing writer, but I never said that I wasn't both. When I read the fine portraits of men and women in *Creative Chicago* who flourished in arts and publishing and education in our city, I find myself concluding that we are not soon to see their like again. When is the world likely again to turn up so extraordinary a woman as

Harriet Monroe, cultivated and liberated in the only sense it is worthwhile to be liberated—that is, liberated to be free to appreciate the best the world has to offer—and, at the same time, open to all that was fresh and new in the line of her choosing? For all his faults, which in his essay Henry Regnery does not scamp, is another man of the quality of Robert Hutchins likely to re-occur in a position of American educational leadership in the forseeable future? Are we ever again to have among us an architect with the same courage in his vision and intelligence of expression as Louis Sullivan? Or novelists of the same craftsman-like dignity of Hamlin Garland and Henry Fuller? (Theodore Dreiser, about whom Henry Regnery writes so well, was of course *sui generis*, both as a wretched human being and a magnificently powerful writer.) The answer to all these questions, alas, is not soon, not likely, probably not ever.

Still, the point of *Creative Chicago*, apart from the intrinsic interest of each of its essays, is the quietly but impressively exhortatory one of reminding its readers of the extraordinary men and women who one day walked the streets of this city of Chicago, of their large aspirations, and of their splendid accomplishments.

CREATIVE CHICAGO

Foreword: The Question of Chicago

THE MEN RESPONSIBLE for the founding and early development of Chicago, we must face it, were not idealists or dreamers but meat packers, merchants, land speculators, railroad builders, transit tycoons, men like Gurdon Saltonstall Hubbard, Cyrus McCormick, the Swifts, the Armours, Marshall Field, Potter Palmer, George Pullman, Charles Yerkes. They were prominent among those who pushed through the canal that made Chicago the vital link between the Great Lakes and the vast Mississippi river system, the same key passage that the portage had provided for the Indians, the French Catholic missionaries and the early fur traders. They built the stockyards, the grain elevators, the lumber schooners and the slips for unloading them, then the railroads, factories and steel mills. It was such men of drive and enterprise who made Chicago a great commercial center, a city that came to be dominated in turn by the rich and the powerful.

There were, however, others in Chicago concerned with less earth-shaking matters: writers, editors, book publishers, educators and one architect in particular, Louis Sullivan, a visionary and a writer as well. Their contribution to the life of the city, not always understood or appreciated, is nonetheless real and deserves to be remembered. Even the most crass among its citizenry would concede that a great city like Chicago cannot live by trade alone.

Books were written and published in Chicago from its earliest days, when it was little more than a frontier settlement, and while many have been written and published in Chicago since, Chicago has never been able to establish itself as a literary center. Such writers as George Ade, Ben Hecht, Theodore Dreiser, Hamlin Garland and Sherwood Anderson were all attracted to Chicago, wrote in Chicago, were influenced by Chicago and took something of Chicago with them when they left, but leave they all did. In spite of numerous valiant efforts to establish a general publishing firm in the city, the leading American publishers remained centered in New York. While Louis Sullivan was recognized and much admired in Europe, after the 1893 World's Fair Chicago ignored him. From

1900 to his death, the only local commission he received was to design the front of a small music store.

In fairness, Chicago has always been, has always had to be, a practical city, digging itself out of the swamp at the joining of the Chicago River and Lake Michigan where fortune had placed it, struggling to survive Indian massacre, frantic land dealing, financial panic, Civil War, and, after rebuilding from the devastating Great Fire of 1871, trying to make its way as an emerging metropolis in the ruthlessly competitive world of nineteenth- and twentieth-century America.

Chicago may not have recognized the genius of Louis Sullivan, nor to have paid much attention to such writers in its midst as Hamlin Garland and Theodore Dreiser, not even to have been aware that it was the home of the leading literary magazine of its time, *The Dial*. Still it must be remembered that the city had another side other than business, and that it took in and provided a life for millions of newcomers, even at a time when it was undertaking the immense task of making a place for itself in the world. The New Englanders, who founded the city and gave it qualities it has never lost, may not have received with much enthusiasm the Irish and German immigrants who came flocking to the city in the 1840s, bringing strange habits and customs, but they did take them in and provide the means to start a new life, as it was to do for the Poles, Czechs, Jews, Italians, Lithuanians and all the others who followed, Jane Addams' Hull House becoming a symbol of the community they sought.

It is characteristic of Chicago that during World War II when the Japanese interned on the West Coast were released, Chicago was one of the few cities willing to accept them, to its great advantage as it turned out, since they quickly became productive and useful members of the city. New York and Philadelphia would have none of them. Tolerance, of course, can degenerate into indifference, but Chicago's quality of acceptance of others is one of its better attributes. This was not much in evidence, it must be admitted, during the race riots of 1919, still it is a characteristic that has made it possible to produce a thriving and viable city of what might appear to be a hopeless mixture of races, national origins, and differing cultural traditions.

The principal cultural institutions of Chicago, the Art Institute, Field Museum, the Chicago Symphony, Newberry Library and the University of Chicago, were all founded in the years between the Great Fire of 1871 and the turn of the century, largely by members or descendants of the New England families who had taken a decisive part in establishing the city. The question reasonably follows: If the means to establish such institutions were available, why not the far more modest support for the enterprises that would have made it possible for Chicago to keep its authors and become a literary center? *The Dial*, which became the leading literary magazine in the country, was founded in Chicago in 1880 by Francis Browne, who came from New England, but seems never to have been given much recognition or support by the people of Chicago. When it was taken to New York in 1919 Chicago seems to have paid no attention whatever. *The Dial*, it would seem, was regarded not as a cultural asset, but just another small business.

At the time of the 1893 World's Fair, three book publishing firms were established in Chicago, of which Stone & Kimball, later to become Herbert S. Stone & Co., was the most successful and lasted the longest, until 1906. There appear to have been ample resources in the Stone family to have provided the necessary financial backing and the business management that young Herbert Stone needed. His father, Melville Stone, who had founded the *Chicago Daily News* and, after selling that newspaper to Victor Lawson, had gone on to launch the Associated Press, apparently decided that a book publishing firm was not a prudent place for the family's assets. Stone's mother, who came from one of the early and most successful merchant families of Chicago, may also have become concerned about the financial situation and prospects of the firm. As members of Chicago's cultural elite, the Stones, it is certain, generously supported the cultural institutions of the city, but it is equally sure that as members of the commercial elite they did not think it appropriate to be involved in such a business venture as book publishing, however significant it may have been as a cultural influence. To reach a proper balance between the requirements of business on one hand and cultural life on the other would take, it would seem, another generation or two.

Willa Cather

In the early 1920s H. L. Mencken announced in his usual self-confident way that Chicago had become "the literary capital of the United States." This gave enormous satisfaction to the local citizens, but whether he meant it seriously seems doubtful. It is more likely that what he wanted was to draw attention to the Chicago realists, Theodore Dreiser, Sherwood Anderson, Edgar Lee Masters, Henry Fuller, Floyd Dell, George Ade, but whether "literary capital" or not, Chicago did for a time produce some outstanding writers. By 1925 they were all gone. The "Chicago renaissance," like an earlier literary flowering at the time of the city's first World's Fair, was short-lived. These outbursts of creativity are puzzling. What brought them about, why did the writers leave, and why have there been no recurrences lately?

The rebuilding of the city after the disaster of the Great Fire, the determination to stage a World's Fair and to attract the world's attention, may have sparked the first burst of literary creativity and Chicago, during the years from 1910 to the 1929 crash, had a number of qualities that could have stimulated writers. It had become a confident, wonderfully colorful, uninhibited city. It was during this time, too, that the darkest side of Chicago claimed attention. Between the Great War and the Great Depression came the Jazz Age, the era of prohibition, the heyday of the bootlegger, the gangster, the crooked politician, when a crime commission called Chicago the most completely corrupt city in the country. Despite all this, the city still had a degree of stability and coherence coming from the continuing influence of its founding families and from its strictly orthodox, strong-willed Catholic cardinal. *The Dial*, to be sure, had gone to New York and there was no literary magazine to replace it, but its influence may have lingered on. In any case, Chicago could still in those day boast *Poetry* magazine and several literate newspapers.

In his memoirs, *A Life With the Printed Word*, John Chamberlin, who at this time was writing daily book reviews for *The New York Times*, remarks, "American literature of the 20th century grew and prospered in the day of the newspaper critic." Then speaking specifically of Chicago, he goes on to say, "The newspaper critics in Chicago—Francis Hackett, Floyd Dell, Burton Roscoe, and Harry

Hansen—were the trumpet voices that brought novelists such as Sherwood Anderson and poets such as Carl Sandburg to the attention of New York publishers."

Women writers, as well, found Chicago a theme for their material. Willa Cather, for example, wrote three Chicago-based novels, the most famous of which was *The Song of the Lark* (1915), a novel about young Thea Kronborg studying music in Chicago in the era of Chicago Symphony Orchestra founder, Theodore Thomas. Cather followed it in 1925 with *The Professor's Umbrella*, about life on campus just north of the city and in 1935 with *Lucy Gayheart*, about a Nebraska girl's sobering experiences in Chicago.

Edna Ferber complained that she was "practically never thought of as having written anything about Chicago" and said just the opposite was true. She had researched the city and written of its history as well as of her era. More than a dozen of her usually excellent short stories had Chicago as a setting as did at least four of her novels: *Fanny Herself* (1917), *The Girls* (1921), *So Big* (1924) and *Show Boat* (1926). So did two of her plays: *The Eldest* and *Minick*.

So Big won the Pulitzer Prize, as did the Margaret Ayer Barnes *Years of Grace* (1930). Other 1930s novels by Barnes included: *Within the Present* (1933), *Edna, His Wife* (1935) and *Wisdom's Gate* (1938.)

It is perhaps too simplistic to decide that a city driven mostly by trade and industry, obsessed by business, overly concerned with commerce, has no room for the creative spirit to make other than sporadic appearances. Still the specter of Shakespeare's character, Caliban, does come to mind, the slave who had to do all the work on Prospero's isle, a symbol of all those who cannot look beyond their labors, who become unimaginative materialists who know everything and understand nothing of this world, suggesting a city of philistines.

The following informal studies—it would be too much to call them essays—were written over a period of years and for different occasions, as articles for the quarterly *Modern Age* or as readings before the Chicago Literary Club. All are concerned, one way or

Edna Ferber

another, with the doers, the dreamers and the clash of cultures in Chicago. While putting them together, the questions persisted: Why, despite its central location at the crossroads of the nation, capital of its heartland, despite its deserved pride in its unparalleled economic progress, despite the many efforts to establish magazines and publishing houses, and above all, despite the many writers it attracted over the years, why had Chicago never become a literary center? And lastly, sadly, despite its great heart and good spirit, how could Chicago have turned its back on that authentic genius, Louis Sullivan, the father of modern architecture, at the peak of his creative success?

There may be no answers to these questions, but certainly the effort to penetrate them can offer the opportunity to encounter again as unlikely a city and as colorful a citizenry as ever appeared in the course of history, a review rewarding in itself, regardless of its outcome.

PART ONE

Book Publishing
in Chicago,
1840 to 1940

Robert Fergus:
A Prophetic Figure

THE FIRST BOOK published in Chicago, according to Alfred T. Andreas' *A History of Chicago*, was *The Public and General Statute Laws of the State of Illinois* issued in 1839. The publisher was Stephen F. Gates, who had arrived in Chicago in 1835 and opened the town's first bookshop. Also published in 1839, when the population of the settlement was only about 4,000, was *The Laws and Ordinances of the City of Chicago*. Because the printer, Robert Fergus, newly arrived in Chicago from Glasgow, had six blank pages at the end, he filled them with a city directory, which was apparently compiled from memory. The first volume of poetry to be printed in Chicago, Horatio Cooke's *Gleanings of Thought*, appeared in 1841, "just six years," as Madelaine B. Stern puts it in an essay on Robert Fergus, "after the Indians had danced their last great dance in what was to become a city, just seven years after the last wild bear had been killed in a wilderness soon to be identified as a city street." In 1843 the printers of these two books, Ellis & Fergus, brought out a poem, *Knowledge is Power*, by William H. Bushnell, and the first complete city directory, which also included "a historical sketch and statistical account of the present time." This city directory is said to be "the first book compiled, printed, bound and issued in Chicago."

The first publishers in Chicago, and this was the general pattern everywhere at this time, were either printers like Robert Fergus, who now and again brought out books under their own name, or booksellers. Among the latter was W. W. Barlow & Co., founded in 1844, which published its first book, *The Prairie Farmer Almanac*, in 1846. Two years later Barlow & Co. became S. C. Griggs & Co., still primarily a bookseller. The next year, 1849, Griggs & Co. published its first book, *History of Medical Education and Institutions in the U.S.* and in 1854 Thomas Ford's *History of Illinois*. As the city grew, and with it the demand for school books, Griggs became the Chicago outlet and eventually co-publisher with several eastern publishers of school texts. A. C. McClurg joined the firm in 1859, by which time it had become the leading bookseller in Chicago.

During the first period of its development, from the 1840s, when the first books were published, until the Great Fire of 1871, an active and vigorous book trade grew up in Chicago, including several firms still in existence. M. A. Donohue was founded in 1861 and by 1866 William H. Rand had set up a printing shop. In 1869 Rand entered into a partnership with Andrew McNally. Other publishers active during this period, all primarily booksellers, were Patrick T. Sherlock, who published a *History of Chicago* by Elias Colbert; Culver, Page & Hoyne; D. B. Cooke; Sherwood & Co.; and E. B. Meyers. The most ambitious project undertaken by a Chicago publisher was *The Mississippi Valley: Its Physical Geography, including Sketches of its Topography, Botany, Climate, Geology and Mineral Resources and the Progress of Development in the Population and Material Wealth*. This was published in 1869 by S. C. Griggs in Chicago and by Trübner in London, and printed in Chicago by Church, Goodman & Donnelley.

The early Chicago printer, Robert Fergus, during his long career also published a number of books of historic interest. Fergus deserves attention not only for what he accomplished but also because the fate of his firm was rather similar to that of many Chicago publishers.

Robert Fergus was born in Glasgow in 1815 and arrived, as mentioned earlier, in Chicago in 1839. He was a well-trained printer, having served and finished his apprenticeship with two leading Scottish printers. He had gone first to Milwaukee at the suggestion of Francis Metcalf, a young Englishman he had met in Glasgow, and although he was offered the choice of a place in his business by Metcalf or a half-interest in the newly founded *Milwaukee Sentinel*, he decided to go on to Chicago. After working as a printer in several different shops, he entered into a partnership with William Ellis. One of their first books was the *General Directory of Chicago*, cited above, which was published in 1844. In the same year, Ellis & Fergus printed and, it may be assumed, published Mrs. Kinzie's *Narrative of the Massacre at Chicago, August 15, 1812*, a thirty-four-page pamphlet with printed wrappers and a frontispiece map of the settlement. The firm also printed *The Illinois Medical and Surgical Journal* for the newly founded Rush Medical College, as well as lectures, announcements and catalogs for that institution. William Ellis left Chicago during the California gold rush and, in 1849, Fergus was burned out twice, which seems not to have been an unusual occurrence for early Chicago business firms. He was forced to work as a compositor for two years to get back on his feet, but by 1852 was again operating his own shop.

The Great Fire of 1871 wiped out not only the business of Robert Fergus, everything he had accumulated during the previous thirty years, but every other printer and bookseller in the city. However, the great Chicago fire was one of those disasters about which it is difficult to decide what is more remarkable: the event itself or the remarkable recovery from it. Within nineteen days after the conflagration, S. C. Griggs & Co. managed to bring out an account of the fire, Elias Colbert's and Everett Chamberlin's *Chicago and the Great Conflagration*, which doubtless had better sales in cities other than Chicago, and, apparently for the Chicago market, *Seed-Time and Harvest*. Fergus, having survived two previous fires, seems to have recovered fairly rapidly. Because so much of the early history of the city had been lost, he made up his mind, in the words of Madelaine Stern, to "rescue from complete oblivion the early history of a city that had gone down in flames. During the forties he had helped make that history. Now, during the seventies and eighties, he would help record it, reminding the world of beginnings that were lost to sight and might otherwise have been lost to memory."

During the next twenty years some thirty issues of his Fergus Historical Series were published. The first was Joseph N. Balestier's *Annals of Chicago*, a lecture which had originally been given in 1840 before the Chicago Lyceum and published by Fergus' first employer, Edward Rudd. Fergus found the copy from which his edition was set at the Wisconsin State Library. The Fergus series also included a reprint of Mrs. Kinzie's *Narrative*, biographical sketches of early Chicago settlers, reminiscences, accounts of the early practice of law and medicine, and papers of the Chicago Historical Society, of which Fergus was a member. The series appeared originally as pamphlets with colored wrappers and sold for 25¢ to $1.50 per copy. They were well printed on ordinary paper, and many were illustrated. One of the last of the series was a reprint of the Chicago City Directory of 1843, which Fergus had first printed at the age of twenty-nine. He wrote the introduction for the reprint on his eighty-first birthday. Fergus was primarily a printer, and he published the Fergus Historical Series more as a labor of love, to preserve as much as he could of the history of the city he had helped to build, than as a business enterprise. He was killed June 23, 1897 by a train during a blinding rainstorm at the south Evanston crossing.

Robert Fergus had been joined in his business by several sons and a grandson, but the business did not long survive him. In 1900, by a writ of ejectment, the stock and equipment were removed from the building the firm had occupied. As a newspaper reported the incident at the time, "the mountain of jumbled printing furniture and paper stock that clogged Michigan Street was a sight to stir the heart to pity." In the rich, prosperous city that Chicago had become during the sixty years Robert Fergus had devoted to serving it and recording its history, there was no one willing to rescue his old firm, and all that it had represented for the city, from an ignominious end.

By the time of the fire, S. C. Griggs & Co. had become the largest bookseller in Chicago as well as the leading publisher. Alexander McClurg had joined the firm in 1859 and, after returning from the Civil War as a brigadier general, took an active and vigorous part in the business. After the fire, the former partnership was dissolved into S. C. Griggs & Co., publishers, and Jansen, McClurg & Co., which opened a bookstore. In 1873, one year after its founding, Jansen, McClurg & Co. published its first book, *Landscape Architecture*, by H. W. S. Cleveland, and two years later one of its most successful books, Max Müller's *Memories: A Story of a German Love*, which was still in print fifty years later. William Bross' *History of Chicago* and David Starr Jordan's *Manual of the Vertebrates*, the latter reprinted many times during the next twenty-five years, were both published in 1876. Four years later the firm began wholesaling books, which eventually became its chief business, and in 1886 the name was changed to A. C. McClurg & Co. By 1880 the publishing end of the business had become sufficiently large to justify the publication of a literary magazine, *The Dial*, which was started as a monthly and published by McClurg's until 1892, when it was sold to its founder and editor, Francis Fisher Browne. Most of the titles published during the 1890s were either U.S. editions of English authors or translations. Two particular successes were the *Law of Psychic Phenomena* by Thomas Jay Hadson (1892), in print for many years, and Elizabeth Wormley Latimer's popular histories of Europe. The firm published one book by Eugene and Roswell Field, a translation of Horace's *Echoes from the Sabine Farm*.

In 1899 the firm was completely burned out for the third time since its founding. It was reorganized as a corporation in 1900, all of the stock being subscribed by employees. There was little publishing until 1914, when McClurg's launched the first book of a series of the sort every publisher dreams of having on his list, Edgar Rice Burroughs' *Tarzan of the Apes*. McClurg's published eleven Tarzan titles in all, selling millions of copies, until Burroughs set up his own firm to capitalize on his success. In 1923 the McClurg bookstore at 218 S. Wabash, which for many years had been a landmark in Chicago and a gathering place for people interested in books, was sold to Brentano's in New York. In 1933 it was acquired by Adolph Kroch. The Kroch & Brentano's bookstore, therefore, by a sort of "apostolic succession," goes back to one of the first bookstores founded in Chicago in 1844, W. W. Barlow & Co., followed by Griggs, Janson-McClurg, A. C. McClurg, Brentano's, and finally, Kroch & Brentano's. The old firm of McClurg, which traced its history to the earliest days of Chicago and had contributed substantially to the development of the book trade and the city's cultural life, as well as the entire Midwest, was finally liquidated in 1962.

From the Great Fire to the turn of the century, Chicago became one of the principal centers of the printing industry. There was also considerable book publishing, but most of the activity was in subscription books and inexpensive reprints. Except for McClurg's, there was little original publishing of trade books—of books, that is, for sale in bookstores. Between 1875 and 1879, Donnelley, Lloyd & Co. published the Lakeside Library of non-copyrighted fiction, selling for as little as 10¢ per copy and including such authors as Scott, Dickens and Cooper. This series was discontinued in 1879. The following year the firm started the Fireside Library, a twenty-four-volume series bound in cloth of such popular authors as Wilkie Collins, Anthony Trollope, and Charles Reade. In 1883 the firm became R. R. Donnelley & Co. and has since become better known as printers than publishers.

Rand, McNally, which early in its career concentrated on printing for the then-booming railroads—tickets, time-tables, maps— in the 1880s began to publish paper-bound editions of popular authors to be sold on trains and in stations. It was called the Globe Library and grew to 170 titles. A similar series, but better produced, called Rialto Books, appeared a little later and by 1892 included fifty titles. One of the more successful subscription book publishers of the time was Belford, Clark & Co., who, in 1885, sold 75,000 sets of their fifteen-volume Dickens. They were also the original publishers of *Peck's Bad Boy*. The firm was discontinued in 1892.

The subscription publishers concentrated on dictionaries, encyclopedias, self-help books and other popular books which were sold by agents. They brought books, often useful and instructive books, to people who would not otherwise have had them. Some of Mark Twain's books—*Huckleberry Finn*, for one—were first published in this fashion. Haines Brothers, another Chicago subscription publisher of this period, seems to have specialized in "success books" like *Worth and Wealth* and *The Genius of Industry*, both issued in 1884. The latter was described as "a valuable and unique treatise on the philosophy of business, or how to get, save and use money." Subscription publishing found Chicago an advantageous location, no doubt because of the excellent facilities for manufacturing and distributing books. Still Chicago, as a center for original publishing, could make no claim to rival New York, Boston or Philadelphia.

A firm that fit none of the standard categories of publishing, at least in its original form, and that brought out many important books is the Open Court Publishing Co., founded in Chicago in 1887 by E. C. Hegeler of LaSalle, Illinois. From its founding until his death in 1919, it was managed by Paul Carus, who, besides publishing such philosophical classics as Locke, Berkeley, Hobbes, Kant, Fichte, Descarte and Leibnitz (the latter in new translations), books on mathematics, philosophy and eastern religions (some written by Carus himself), managed also to bring out two scholarly magazines, the *Monist* devoted to the philosophy of science and *The Open Court* devoted to the science of religion. The purpose of all this, as it was formulated in one of the firm's announcements, was "a reformation of religious life on the basis of science."

After the death of Paul Carus, the firm was less active, but published some important works of contemporary philosophers, including Ernst Cassirer, and kept its series of philosophical classics in print in their inexpensive, paper-bound editions. The magazines were discontinued in the 'thirties, when the office was moved to LaSalle. Now, under the direction of a grandson of Carus, M. Blouke Carus, the firm has resumed active publishing, with a children's magazine, *Cricket*, an innovative series of phonic readers, and a substantial trade list.

Stone & Kimball *and* The Chap-Book

ONE OF THE MOST CREATIVE and imaginative publishers ever to operate in Chicago was Stone & Kimball and its successor, Herbert S. Stone & Co. An excellent and complete history of the firm by Sidney Kramer, originally written as a doctoral thesis and beautifully published by Norman Forgue, is the source of much of what follows.

Herbert Stuart Stone was born in Chicago in 1871, the son of Melville Elijah Stone who came from a family of Methodist ministers. When the foundry the elder Stone had recently purchased was destroyed in the Great Fire, he went into journalism and, in 1875, founded the *Chicago Daily News*. He retired from the newspaper in 1888 to travel in Europe, taking his family with him. While editor of the *Daily News*, Melville Stone brought Eugene Field to Chicago and he became a close friend of the family. This familiarity with a popular writer was undoubtedly stimulating to the son and also helpful to his later career in publishing. Herbert Stone entered Harvard in 1890 at the age of nineteen, after a year or two of schooling in Europe. Hannibal Ingalls Kimball was three years younger than Stone, but he entered Harvard in the same class. He was born in Massachusetts, but had been educated largely in the South, where his father had gone soon after the Civil War as the southern representative of the Pullman Company. Kimball senior was an aggressive, successful businessman and some of his talent and drive seems to have been inherited by his son.

Stone's first venture in publishing was *Chicago and the World's Fair: A Popular Guide*, which he wrote and illustrated himself. He met Kimball when both were on the staff of the Harvard *Crimson*, and the partnership of Stone & Kimball was organized in 1893. The first publications of the new firm appeared soon after: a reprint of the *Guide* and a book which Stone had compiled and for which Eugene Field had written an introduction: *First Editions of American Authors*. They brought out their first impressive list in the fall of that year, which included books by Eugene Field, Hamlin Garland, Joaquin Miller, and Kenneth Grahame. In May of the following year, 1894, the first issue of their magazine, *The Chap-Book*, made its appearance and was an instant success. All of this was done, it should be remembered, while both were Harvard undergraduates. There was some objection from the school authorities because of the effect such strenuous activity was having on their college work, but Stone, who from all accounts was an extremely persuasive and charming young man, was able to convince the dean that they should be given the same academic consideration as football players, since what they were doing would be of equal credit and honor to the university.

The work of Stone & Kimball, it seems fair to say, reflected the esthetic movement of the 1890s. It was doubtless their identification with the idealism and esthetic aspirations of their contemporaries and their skill in expressing the spirit of the times which explains the really phenomenal, immediate success of their foray into publish-

Herbert Stuart Stone

ing. It also explains its short life. They were young and inexperienced, but such an adventure as they undertook could only have been attempted by men who were young, idealistic, and unfamiliar with the hard realities of the marketplace. They soon ran into such inescapable barriers as balance sheets and operating statements but their real interest, as their careers demonstrate, was in breaking new paths and establishing new standards of excellence, and in this they were eminently successful.

The first number of their magazine, *The Chap-Book*, appeared May 15, 1894, was published twice a month, consisted of twenty four pages, 7½" by 4½", and cost a nickel. As the magazine itself explained in a later issue, the term "chap-books" referred to the small, cheaply made, popular books, often illustrated with rather crude woodcuts, which were sold by pedlars in eighteenth- and early nineteenth-century England. "They took their name from the pedlar, or Chapman, who, carrying them, with other goods, wandered from village to village, from farmhouse to farmhouse an ever welcome guest, who could retail the latest news of the countryside, and whose pack carried an *omnium gatherum* of delights, unattainable except by a visit to the market town."

The first issue announced as well that "*The Chap-Book* will have at least one signed review in nearly every number, besides several short notices and literary essays." Further, *The Chap-Book* "will contain poems and occasional short stories by both well-known and unknown writers." In a letter to his family, perhaps to calm their nerves, Stone wrote, "To speak plainly, *The Chap-Book* is no more nor less than a semi-monthly advertisement and regular prospectus for Stone & Kimball." Their success, in speaking for their contemporaries, is attested not only by the immediate critical acclaim for their magazine, but also by the large number of imitations that sprang up all over the country. Most, it is sad to note, disappearing as quickly as they had arisen. Kansas City was especially prolific with four: *The Baton*, *The Lotus*, *Pierrot* and *Poster Lore*. Even Wheeling, West Virginia, had a "dinky magazine," as they were called, as did San Antonio, Salt Lake City, New York, Portland and Washington. H. L. Mencken was later to call this eruption the "pianissimo revolt of the 'nineties.'" By the end of its first year, *The*

Hannibal Ingalls Kimball

Chap-Book had expanded to thirty-six pages from the original twenty-four and had an average circulation for the previous three months of 12,206.

The Chap-Book soon established a definite place for itself and became much more than "a semi-monthly advertisement for Stone & Kimball," although its excellence and originality no doubt attracted both attention and authors to the firm. Almost as well known as the magazine itself were the *art nouveau* posters that were produced to advertise it, including one by Toulouse-Lautrec, which were sold separately and soon became collectors' items. Just one hundred issues of the magazine appeared during its life from May 15, 1894 to July 1, 1898; the original small format was kept until the issue of January 15, 1897, when the size was increased to 11" by 14". For the first two years the covers follow the same rather formal design—a black border around the name and contents of the magazine, which are in black and red, set in Caslon old-style type. Toward the end of 1895 the publishers began to use different covers, sometimes drawings, but always in unobtrusive good taste.

After more than seventy-five years, the issues of the magazine, especially those of the first two or three years, have a wonderfully appealing quality of high spirits and of pleasure in the better things of life. The first number, besides poetry, a story and a literary essay, includes announcements of the forthcoming publications of Stone & Kimball: their ten-volume, complete edition of Poe; twelve essays on art, *Crumbling Walls*, by Hamlin Garland; and a book of lyrics, *Low Tide on Grand Pré*, by Bliss Carmen. Among contributors to later issues were Charles T. Copeland, Ralph Adams Cram, Eugene Field, Henry James, H. G. Wells, Max Beerbohm, Paul Verlaine, George Santayana, Joseph Pennell. There were frequent illustrations by Aubrey Beardsley. A further attractive feature of *The Chap-Book* were the "Notes" that appeared in most issues—comments by the editors on art and literature, interspersed with amusing little anecdotes, all reflecting, but without a trace of pomposity or arrogance, their own strongly held esthetic views and sense of mission. There was also a fair amount of advertising for soap and bicycles, by railroads for their passenger service, and as time went on, by other publishers, showing that the magazine was taken seriously and had a readership worth reaching. *The Chap-Book*, it must be said, from the very first issue gotten out by two Harvard undergraduates, was a thoroughly professional performance and a high point in the history of Chicago publishing.

The following comments on Gilbert Parker and Rudyard Kipling from the "Notes" of the fourth issue of the magazine indicate rather clearly the attitude of the two young publishers toward literature:

> The glamor of poetry has not passed from earth for these men; they are still adventurers and dreamers, with an unfailing zest for the marvelous drama of men and women. The tame doings of un-ventful lives seem hardly worth relating, and there is no interest in recording their monotonous small talk. These tale tellers, these re-viewers of the genuine story-telling, have set their face against the passing fashion of realism; and there are many readers who will welcome them as a godsend. After the dreary wastes of all our un-imaginative preachers, with their "ethical purpose in art," their "realism," their "veritism," their "naturalism," and Heaven knows what clap-trap beside, a good round wholesome lie, a splendid un-believable fabric of events that never happened and hardly could happen, is as refreshing as a sea-wind through city streets in sum-mer time.

Robert Louis Stevenson, not surprisingly, was very much to the taste of the editors of *The Chap-Book*, who, in the issue of March 1, 1895, published not long after his death a delightful reminiscence by Eve Balantyre Simpson, whose brother had accompanied Steven-son on the canoe trip described in *Inland Voyage*. The following from her remembrance of Stevenson is rather characteristic in tone and spirit of *The Chap-Book*:

> After *The Inland Voyage*, Louis was full of a project to buy a barge and saunter through the canals of Europe, Venice being the far-off terminus. A few select shareholders in this scheme were chosen, mostly artists, for the barge plan was projected in the mellow autumnal days at Fontainebleau Forest, where artists abounded. Robert A. Stevenson, Louis's cousin, then a wielder of the brush, was to be of the company. He, too, though he came of

the shrewd Scottish civil engineer stock, had, like his kinsman, a foreign look and a strong touch of Bohemianism in him. He, also, with these alien looks, had his cousin's attractive power of speech and fertile imagination. The barge company were then all in the hey-day of their youth. They were to paint fame-enduring pictures, as they leisurely sailed through life and Europe, and when bowed, grey-bearded, bald-headed men, they were to cease their journeyings at Venice. There, before St. Mark's, a crowd of clamorously eager picture dealers and lovers of art were to be waiting to purchase the wonderful work of the wanderers. The scene in the piazza of St. Marks on the barge's arrival, and the excited throng of anxious buyers, the hoary-headed artists, tottering under the weight of canvases, was pictured in glowing colors by their author, when the forest was smelling of the "ripe breath of autumn." The barge was purchased, but bankruptcy presently stared its shareholders in the face.

In August 1894, a few months after the launching of *The Chap-Book*, the firm was moved from Cambridge to Chicago. The office of the company was located in the Caxton building on South Dearborn Street, at that time close to the printing and publishing district, and it soon became a gathering place for residents of the city interested in art and literature. Harrison Garfield Rhodes, a fellow student at Harvard who had joined the partners when still in Cambridge as assistant editor of *The Chap-Book*, also came to Chicago, and as editor and reader, contributed substantially to the success of the firm. In an account written many years later, and probably somewhat colored by the passing of time, Hamlin Garland wrote the following description of the impression made by the three young publishers after their arrival in Chicago: ". . . when, of an afternoon these three missionaries of culture each in a long frock coat tightly buttoned, with cane, gloves and shining silk hats, paced side by side down the Lake Shore Drive they had the effect of an esthetic invasion, but their crowning audacity was a printed circular which announced that tea would be served in their office on Saturday afternoons . . . Culture on the Middle Border had at last begun to hum!"

They were three young men who not only had a strong sense of mission and high standards in literature and design, but, there seems every reason to believe, enormously enjoyed what they were doing. Tea *was* served in their office on Saturday afternoons, as Garland said, and there were other forms of pleasant entertainment as well: "public readings of manuscripts," according to Kramer, "book and picture exhibitions, 'Chap-Book teas' and Vaudevilles." They very quickly made themselves a lively and much appreciated addition to the life of the city, and gave it something which was long remembered and often spoken of.

They also worked hard—in the year and one half after their move to Chicago, besides getting out *The Chap-Book* twice a month, they published some forty five books, including their ten-volume, beautifully produced, complete edition of Poe, which is still considered the standard edition; *The Land of Heart's Desire* by William Butler Yeats; Stevenson's *Ebb Tide, Macaire, Vailima Letters*, and *The Amateur Emigrant; The Golden Age* by Kenneth Grahame; *The Plays of Maurice Maeterlinck*; Ibsen's last play, *Little Eyolf; Poems* of Paul Verlaine; Laurence Stern's *Tristam Shandy*; and Hamlin Garland's *Rose of Dutcher's Coolly*. Early in 1896 they brought out the most successful book published under the Stone & Kimball imprint, Harold Frederic's *The Damnation of Theron Ware*, which soon went to 20,000 copies. A larger office was taken in the Caxton building on March 1, 1896, and a New York office was opened by Kimball. But the publication of the Poe had overstrained their capital, apparently, and raising the advance of $2,900 for Stevenson's *Ebb Tide* and the option on his further work, led to differences between the two partners. When Stone's father demanded liquidation of some of the firm's titles to ease the financial strain, Kimball in April 1896 made an offer to buy Stone's interests, which was accepted, with the result that everything but *The Chap-Book* went with him to New York.

Kimball went on to publish thirty six titles in New York and his books maintained the highest standards, but he was terribly short of cash and was soon in financial difficulties. He had to sell the last two Stevenson titles left after the author's death, the unfinished novels *Weir of Hermiston* and *St. Ives*, the former already in type, to

Scribner's, and on October 21, 1897, the firm was liquidated at public auction. Herbert Stone in the meantime had been joined by his younger brother, Melville E. Stone, Jr., and had set up the new firm of Herbert S. Stone & Co. At the auction of the Stone & Kimball assets, the Stones bought most of the copyrights, plates and unbound stock, and were, therefore, in every respect the successors to Stone & Kimball.

The new firm continued *The Chap-Book* and began an active book list, the first authors for the most part being contributors to *The Chap-Book*, plus a book of travel sketches by H. C. Chatfield-Taylor and a novel by Gabriele D'Annunzio. In 1897 and 1898 the firm published, among other books, Henry James's *What Maisie Knew* and three books by George Ade, *Artie*, *Pink Marsh* and *'Doc' Horne*, all collections made at Herbert Stone's suggestion from the column, "Stories of the Streets and the Town," that Ade had been writing since 1890 for the *Chicago Record*. A one-volume selection of these stories was published many years later by the Caxton Club.

Stone was an innovative publisher. He became, for example, not only George Bernard Shaw's first American publisher, bringing out his first three plays, two novels and a volume of criticism, but Shaw's first American agent as well. Stone's greatest financial success was George Barr McCutcheon's romantic novel, *Graustark*, published in 1901, which went to 150,000 copies by the end of the year. The book had come into the office as an unsolicited manuscript, it is worth mentioning, having been written while McCutcheon was working on a small newspaper in Indiana. It required considerable editing by the publisher, who also, apparently, drove a rather hard bargain—a member of the McCutcheon family reports that the author got only $500 out of the book. There were two other McCutcheon novels, both successful and both, like the first, skillfully promoted: *Castle Craneycrow* and *Brewster's Millions*. Thereafter the author, as so often happens to Chicago publishers, transferred his allegiance to New York. The same thing happened to George Ade; after the collections mentioned above, all of which were successful, the firm brought out two collections of his *Fables in Slang*, the success of which made Ade a national figure and convinced him that he needed a New York publisher.

In 1898 Herbert S. Stone & Co. moved into a new office, a rebuilt carriage house at the rear of the old Willoughby mansion at Michigan and Twelfth Streets. It must have been an attractive place—fireplaces, brick floors, deep yellow walls, dark green woodwork, a picket fence and a row of sunflowers to screen off the outside world. It also became, like its predecessor, a gathering place for the literati of the day. This move seems to have come at the crest of the fortunes of Herbert S. Stone & Co.; in 1899, the following year, the firm published from its new quarters a total of fifty new books, which placed the company among the larger American publishers. The prior year Stone had also taken over the publication list of Way and Williams, a Chicago firm that had, since starting out in 1894, published twenty six handsome books, several designed by Bruce Rogers. Two years after this acquisition, however, Stone sold the list to Doubleday & McClure in New York, apparently to raise additional capital, and in 1900 the number of newly published books began to decline sharply—only thirty new books in 1900 appeared, down from the fifty in the previous year; and in the five-year period from 1901 to 1905, there were only thirty seven new titles issued.

In 1898, the year of the outbreak of the Spanish-American War, the publication of *The Chap-Book* was discontinued. It was in that same year that Harrison Garfield Rhodes left Chicago to live in London, where, besides representing several American newspapers, he was to keep in touch with English publishers on behalf of Herbert S. Stone & Co. Rhodes was much respected as a discerning critic, and had undoubtedly contributed substantially to the success of *The Chap-Book*, with which he had been closely connected from the beginning, and to the high standards of both Stone & Kimball and Herbert S. Stone & Co. During the last year or two of its existence, the editors of *The Chap-Book* obviously struggled with the problem of making a "dinky" magazine that expressed the exuberance and rebelliousness against conventions of its youthful founders into a more or less conventional literary journal. The format, with the issue of January 15, 1897, was increased to a larger size, as has been noted, and the descriptive subtitle changed from "A Semi-Monthly" to the more prepossessing "A Miscellary & Review of Belles Lettres." The "Notes" changed their tone entirely, from observations on contemporary literary fashions or amusing anecdotes to rather ponderous comments on the political issues of the day—free silver, the situation in Cuba, the various political candidates. Most of the magazine's space, however, was still devoted to stories, essays, and serious well-written book reviews. The magazine was still attractively designed and well printed, but the light-heartedness was gone. One has the distinct impression of fading fortune especially when, with the issue of February 15, 1898, the paper stock was changed from unfinished to glossy, so that half-tones could be used. Half-tone illustrations of American admirals who had defeated the outgunned Spanish were completely out of character and soon after their appearance, the issue of *The Chap-Book* of July 1, 1898 was announced as its last. No matter how much they may have tried to accommodate themselves to the spirit of the times, the editors were not, it seems safe to say, in sympathy with its manifestations—the Spanish-American War, "Manifest Destiny," the Rough Riders, and all the rest. They said as much in an editorial comment in the issue of May 1, 1898: "The sulphurous vomitings of the yellow journals since the blowing-up of the Maine bear out Señor Castelar's recently expressed opinion that nowhere in the world is there a calamity comparable to the American daily press."

The subscription lists of *The Chap-Book* were turned over to *The Dial*, which was still published in Chicago. ". . . it was not felt that it was necessary," the editors told their readers in the last issue, "to continue *The Chap-Book* longer to demonstrate that a good literary magazine could be published in the West, and receive the critical sanction of the whole country. . . . They believe that they have been consistently honest in trying to give their public what seemed to them the best writing they could procure, whether it came from new or well-known authors. They believe, furthermore, that *The Chap-Book* has been the strongest protest we have had in America against the habit of promiscuous over-praise which is threatening to make the whole body of American criticism useless and stultifying."

Stone went on to do some of his most successful and significant book publishing after 1898; George Moore's *Esther Waters* in 1899 and his *Bending of the Bough* in 1900, for example; in addition, the George Ade and George Barr McCutcheon titles, already cited. But as the number of titles began to decline, one has the impression that Stone's own enthusiasm was declining also. In a letter to his mother dated November 2, 1899, he tells her that sales are up and while, with the help of his father, he had just had to "borrow some money from the bank," he was confident that all debts would be paid by January 15th. No financial information, according to Kramer, is available, but in the letter referred to above Stone remarks that sales for 1898 were "44 thousand," and up to November 1, 1899, were $58,067.26. Hardly enough to sustain a national publishing operation even in those days.

Writing again to his mother the following March, Stone is still optimistic, but mentions rather drastic steps being taken to reduce expenses, including the closing of the New York office. In spite of the success of McCutcheon's *Graustark* and *Brewster's Millions*, the drive and enthusiasm necessary for innovative publishing seems to have left him, all the more because the financial stringency he was working under made it necessary to give less and less attention to the proper design of books. "When he had to cut down expenses and could not make the beautiful books he loved, he lost interest," is the way one of his former editors, Lucy Monroe Calhoun, described it.

Stone's last book was published in 1905—it was the only book he published that year—titled *Historic Styles of Furniture*, by his associate on *House Beautiful*, Virginia Robie. It would become a classic in its field, but too late to save the firm. On March 10, 1906, the firm, including copyrights, plates, sheets, goodwill and contracts, was sold to Fox, Duffield & Company of New York. The lists of this firm in turn were sold in 1934 to Dodd, Mead & Co.

It is interesting to consider why this firm, which started so brilliantly and left an indelible mark on bookmaking in this country, should have survived for such a short time, only from 1893 when Stone & Kimball was established by two Harvard undergraduates and published its first book, to 1906 when Herbert S. Stone & Co. was finally sold. Kimball went on to a successful career in advertising layout and printing and Stone prospered as a magazine editor, so it could not have been incompetence. Their careers as publishers, in any case, made it quite evident that while they may have been young and inexperienced, they lacked neither skill, energy nor imagination. They were, in the good sense of the word, amateurs, in that they devoted more attention to producing something that satisfied their own high standards than in appealing to the market. Their beautifully produced books are prized by collectors today and now bring rather high prices, but one can be quite sure that the additional effort that went into making them the outstanding books that they were was not justified from a strictly business point of view. They were always plagued, apparently, by inadequate capital, but it seems likely that with their connections and with the success they had attained, they could have raised the funds they needed if they had been willing to make the concessions that a commercial operation required.

Herbert S. Stone had the problem of every trade publisher who operates in Chicago: namely, that Chicago is not New York. This must have been made strikingly apparent to Stone when his two most successful authors left him for New York publishers, and all the more so in view of the fact that he had made them successful. The reviewers, agents and the magazines were then, as they still are, all in New York. That city is the center from which literary ideas are disseminated in our country. It is the magnet that has an almost irresistible attraction to those who have, or think they have, something to say and the talent to express it. It is true that when Kimball acquired Stone & Kimball and took the firm to New York the move did not help; he lasted for not much more than a year, but this was obviously due to his refusal to make the concessions to the market which a successful commercial publishing operation requires, and above all to his inadequate capitalization. In the last issue of *The Chap-Book*, there is the comment, "*The Chap-Book* has never depended in any special way upon the West for support; indeed, it is probable that in proportion to its size, Chicago has fewer subscribers than any other large city," and one of the last editors of the Chicago *Dial* remarked, after it had been moved to New York, that everyone in Chicago talked about *The Dial*, was proud of it as a local institution, but that very few ever read it.

The reasons cited for the short life of Stone & Kimball and Herbert S. Stone & Co., their refusal, or inability, to make concessions to the demands of the market, inadequate capital, and their location in Chicago, all, no doubt, played their part but the chief reason for their short life may well have been something else. They had outlived their time and their reason for existence. Stone & Kimball, as has been said before, reflected the aspirations and idealism of its time, which undoubtedly was the main reason for their success. By 1905 all this had passed. The esthetic revolt of the 'nineties was a revolt against the extreme materialism and commercialism of the late nineteenth century as well as a revolt against its artistic sterility. It may have been a "revolt in pianissimo" as Mencken called it, but it was no less genuine because it did not involve violence and uproar. When the United States went into the Spanish-American War and annexed the Phillipines, to a large extent because of the popular hysteria created by a venal press, it entered the arena of world power politics; within the next five years Theodore Roosevelt had become president, and U.S. Steel and International Harvester had been organized. The century of the big corporation, of big government, of the big labor unions, of the mass press, of world wars and world depressions had begun. The revolt which Stone & Kimball represented had been passed by, but that in no way detracts either from their aims nor their achievement. They established a measure of quality and integrity in bookmaking that will stand for all time.

From the Oz Books
to Tarzan

A PUBLISHING FIRM that operated on quite a different level than Stone & Kimball, but still deserves mention, is Reilly & Lee, the original publishers of all of the Oz books, except the first, and that "poet of the people," Edgar A. Guest. The firm was founded in 1902 as the Madison Book Company and was planned to be the distributing agency for the Webster Unabridged Dictionary. Frank K. Reilly, the founder and president until his death in the 1930s, had been the sales manager of the George M. Hill Co., which had published L. Frank Baum's *The Wonderful Wizard of Oz*. To the surprise of everyone involved—Baum had had to pay to get the book published at all—it was an immediate success. But the George M. Hill Co. went bankrupt and Bobbs-Merrill in Indianapolis acquired the copyright of the *Wizard*. Reilly, however, had become a friend of Baum, and in 1904 published the second Oz book, the original title of which was *The Marvelous Land of Oz: Further Adventures of the Scarecrow and the Tin Woodsman*. In that year the name of the firm was changed to Reilly & Britton; it did not become Reilly & Lee until 1919. All of Baum's subsequent books were published by Reilly's firm, and there were many besides the Oz books, some written under pseudonyms. Baum became rather bored with Oz, in fact, and with the fifth Oz book, *The Emerald City*, announced that this would be the last and consigned Oz to oblivion. Baum's other books, however, were less successful, and of necessity Oz was revived. Altogether Baum wrote fourteen Oz books, and all of them, as of this writing, are still in print.

An interesting episode in the history of Reilly & Lee is their publication of two books by Joseph Medill Patterson, who later founded the *New York Daily News*, the first in 1908, *A Little Brother of the Rich*, and the second, *Rebellion*, in 1911. They were the product, apparently, of the *Sturm und Drang* years of the author—the catalog description of the first has this to say, "The author, an insider who knows the facts, has written about the *idle* rich and how they spend their time and money; the actress who 'gets ahead' by devious means, the pitfalls which beset the path of the chorus girl and the girl behind the counter."

Reilly & Lee were publishers of wholesome, popular works—books for children, diet and health books, sports and hobby books, and popular novels—those of Harold Bell Wright, for example, which were enormously successful in their day. One Reilly & Lee offering, first published in 1919, *One Hundred and One Famous Poems*, became one of the best-sellers of all time, having sold more than six million copies. It still sells enough each year to put it on the best-seller lists if it were a newly published title.

There was a short period after World War I, it will be remembered, when Chicago appeared to be going through some sort of literary revival. One expression of this was the firm of Pascal Covici. Like most of the others, however, Covici soon moved to New York, still his efforts to establish an outpost of literary publishing in Chicago was a serious one. Covici was born in Rumania, was brought to this country as a child, and, after having been a public relations man for a Florida grapefruit company, he opened a bookshop in the early 'twenties in partnership with William McGee on West Washington Street. McGee was an unfrocked priest from the Pacific Northwest, who ended his career as a Unitarian minister. Their publication list for 1923 under the name Covici-McGee included Maxwell Bodenheim's first novel, *Blackguard*, poetry by Bodenheim and Vincent Starrett, a book of literary essays by Starrett, and several other novels, including *Grey Towers*, author anonymous, which is described as "A novel of protest, written by a young apostle of revolt against the present system of education in the colleges." There was no attempt, this author had discovered, "to relate education to life"—as has often been remarked, things don't change much over time!

Because of some difficulty over an obscenity suit, the bookstore was closed, the firm's name changed to "Pascal Covici, Publisher," and a small office taken above the McClurg store on Wabash Avenue, where it stayed until Covici moved in 1928 to New York.

The Covici books for 1924 listed in the *Publishers' Trade List Annual*, still under the name Covici-McGee Co., included novels by

Henry Justin Smith and Vincent Starrett, books of poetry by Harriet Monroe and by the University of Chicago Poetry Club, the latter with an introduction by Robert Morss Lovett. The last Chicago list came out in 1927 under the name of Pascal Covici, Publisher, and was obviously put together by a professional and intended for a wide variety of tastes. The catalog itself is a good example of fine typography and includes two books by the designer Douglas C. McMurtrie, *The Golden Book*, on the history of fine bookmaking, and *The First Printers of Chicago*. There was Ben Hecht's *1,001 Afternoons in Chicago*, a contemporary French novel translated by Ford Maddox Ford, the "first definitive and complete Petronius in English, elaborately printed and illustrated," the *Secret History of Procopius*, also "now made available for the first time in modern but unexpurgated English," *A Key to the Ulysses of James Joyce*, with a map of Dublin, the first written work of the Marquis de Sade, the *Works of Aretino*, Ezra Pound's *Treatise on Harmony*, several volumes of contemporary poetry, *Gemixte Pickles* in the Katzenjammer Kids' German of Kurt Stein, and *A History of Prostitution*. Something, as can be seen, for every taste. The following year Covici moved to New York and became a member of the firm of Covici-Friede, which survived until 1938, when Covici became chief editor of Viking. The reasons for his move to New York were likely the usual ones: the attraction of the city where active literary life was largely concentrated.

Textbook publishing, which has been an important activity in Chicago for a long time, is really quite a different business than trade book publishing, but something should be said about the University of Chicago Press, which occupies a position somewhere between textbook and tradebook publishing. The University's first president, William Rainey Harper, considered a press to be "an organic part" of the kind of university he had in mind, since a press would be required to make the work of scholarship coming out of the University generally available. The University Press, therefore, was founded almost simultaneously with the University in 1891 and brought out its first books the following year. Three journals founded in those early years are still published—the Press now publishes more than thirty—and one book published before 1900 is still in print, John Dewey's *The School and Society*. When the time came to celebrate the tenth anniversary of the founding of the University, President Harper who felt that nothing would be more appropriate than the publication of books by its scholars, planned three, for which he appropriated $2,000. The project ended up with the publication of twenty eight books and publishing costs of more than $50,000. Among the authors were Robert A. Millican, Albert A. Michelson, Thorstein Veblen, and George Herbert Mead. The size of the deficit nearly wrecked the press, but the project drew the attention of the academic world to what was going on at Chicago, which is what Harper no doubt had in mind.

Since then the University of Chicago Press has become a substantial institution and by far the largest university press in the country. The all-time best-seller published by the Press is *The Complete Bible: An American Translation*, which includes the Goodspeed translation of the New Testament and that of the Old Testament by J. M. Powis Smith. Among the many notable books published by the Press are F. A. Hayek's *Road to Serfdom*, Richard Weaver's *Ideas Have Consequences*, and Erik Voegelin's *The New Science of Politics*. Nor should one forget *A Manual of Style*, which is an essential part of the equipment of every conscientious editor. With its journals and scholarly publishing the University of Chicago Press plays an important role in making the work of American scholarship available throughout the world and is one of the major cultural institutions of Chicago.

It is perhaps inevitable that book publishers are inclined to go where the writers, the agents, the largest publishers, the important book reviewers and the literary magazines are to be found. When questioned some years ago about what had happened to the Chicago writers—Floyd Dell, Carl Sandburg, Francis Hackett, Edgar Lee Masters, Robert Morss Lovett, Ben Hecht, and Sherwood Anderson were all at one time "Chicago writers"—Vincent Starrett remarked: "When the second-hand bookstores begin to go, so do the authors. I think what depresses me most is the lack of the little bookstore. When I first came on the scene in 1905, we used to meet in the bookstores. Authors need places like that to get together." It takes more than authors, of course, to keep bookstores going—

most of all it takes people who buy books. Writers, like all creative people, require a receptive audience, which means not only readers who show some sign of appreciating what writers are trying to do, but intelligent criticism also. There are, of course, many intelligent and critical readers in Chicago, but could Chicago now muster the talent and especially the financial and public support necessary to sustain anything comparable to the *New York Review of Books?* There is certainly no tangible evidence that it could. Another example of the difference between New York and Chicago is the book review section of the Sunday *New York Times*, which probably has more influence in Chicago than all the local reviews combined.

Still there is a tendency to forget that Chicago is a relatively new city and had to surmount the rawest beginnings. Gurdon Hubbard, an early settler, described the place as he first encountered it as "four and a half houses, a fort, and a Potawatami town." Charles J. Latrobe, an English writer, described it as ". . . five thousand Indians collected around a little upstart village." He found collected around the fort "a most motley scene. A little knot of officers, residents, a doctor or two, two or three lawyers, a land agent, five or six hotel keepers and merchants." The locals themselves he described as "birds of passage, horse dealers and horse stealers—rogues of every sort, white, black, brown and red; half-breeds, quarter-breeds, and men of no breed at all; dealers in pigs, poultry and potatoes; creditors, sharpers of every degree, pedlars, grog sellers." Further, he found "the little village in an uproar from morning until night, and from night to morning the Indians howled, sang, wept, yelled and whooped in their encampments."

In an editorial in the old *Freeman*, which was published in New York but financed by a Chicago Swift, Albert J. Nock, declared: "The Great Tradition contemplates a harmonious and balanced development in human society of the instinct of workmanship (the instinct for progressive material well-being, with which industry and trade are concerned), the instinct of intellect and knowledge, the instinct of religion and morals, the instinct of beauty and poetry, the instinct of social life and manners." It has been, it must not be forgotten, little more than a century and a half since "the Indians danced their last great dance" in what has become Chicago; to build a great city in that length of time required a considerable degree of concentration on the "instinct for progressive well-being." This is not to say that the other instincts Nock speaks of were entirely neglected, but as a more balanced relationship is achieved between them all, without undue emphasis on any, perhaps the point will be reached where writers, and publishers also, will not always feel compelled to pack up and go somewhere else.

PART TWO

The Creative Spirit in a Prairie Setting

Francis F. Browne

The Dial
*and Chicago's Saving Remnant**

CHICAGO during the tumultuous years following the Civil War attracted all manner of enterprising people who saw an opportunity in the booming, growing city, some to make money, a few others, among the dozen or so who attempted to launch literary journals, to raise the level of public discourse. Among the latter was Francis F. Browne who arrived in Chicago in 1867 and founded *The Dial*, which became the leading literary magazine in the country.

Like so many others who played a creative part in the development of Chicago, beginning with Gurdon Saltonstall Hubbard who arrived in 1818 at the age of sixteen, Francis Browne came from New England. He was born in South Halifax, Vermont, on December 1, 1843 and taken by his family when he was seven to Chicopee, Massachusetts, where his father ran a newspaper and, to supplement its meagre earnings, also taught school. The boy received what education was available in the local public schools, which, judging from his later accomplishments, must have been sound, and learned the printer's trade and something about the use of words in the shop of his father's paper. In the days before instant, mass communications, such local newspapers, which were the chief source of information and reading matter for many of their patrons, served an important cultural function and were often of high quality. After serving in the Civil War as a volunteer in a Massachusetts regiment, from which he returned with health problems that were to plague him for the rest of his life, Browne took up the study of law, first in a law office in Rochester, New York, and then at the University of Michigan. From Ann Arbor he went back to Rochester, worked for a time in a printing shop, married Susan Seaman Brooks, and in 1867 arrived with his new wife in Chicago.

* With some alterations, this follows a reading given before the Chicago Literary Club, February 3, 1986 and published as Club Paper LXXXX.

Browne came to the city, his son remarked in his obituary, with the hope of getting into periodical publishing in one form or another, and within two years of his arrival bought an interest in a new magazine, the *Western Monthly*, the name of which, after he gained control, he changed to the *Lakeside Monthly*. It was Browne's intention with this magazine to encourage and publish western writers; according to an article in the *Inland Printer* of October 1892, it was soon recognized as one of the four or five best monthlies in the country. Browne managed to survive two fires, the second the conflagration of 1871, plus the financial panic of 1873, but a complete breakdown of his health in 1874, just at the time the magazine was beginning to pay its own way, forced him to discontinue, which must have been a crushing blow. He moved away from Chicago for a time in an effort to regain his health, and for the next six years supported himself and his growing family by writing editorials and articles for various magazines and newspapers and by acting as literary editor of *The Alliance*, at that time a respected and influential weekly. The magazine bug had obviously gotten into his system, and with better health and some six years to think about and plan his next venture, in 1880, with the help of Jansen, McClurg & Co., then the largest book wholesalers in Chicago, he founded *The Dial*, which was to become the leading literary magazine in the country.

The Dial began as a monthly. The first issue of twenty four pages appeared in May, 1880. Jansen, McClurg & Co. is shown as publisher, but the name of the editor does not appear. A one-year subscription was to be had for $1.00 and a single copy for 10¢. The first issue opens with a rather long, scholarly review by W. F. Poole, later librarian of the Newberry Library, of Hildreth's *History of the United States*. Among other books reviewed is Henry Adams' novel *Democracy*, which was published anonymously. It received good marks from *The Dial*, a tribute to the editorial judgment of its editor. The editor himself reviewed a book of poetry by Austin Dobson. Browne was a poet in his own right and a formidable reciter of poetry—he was reputed to have been able to recite from memory all the shorter works of Tennyson, whom he greatly admired, as well as those of Robert Burns and Wordsworth. There are other reviews and a list of books published the previous month, arranged by subject, which became a regular feature of the magazine; at the back of *The Dial* there were five pages of advertisements, mostly for books; it was the advertising, for which Browne had the influence of Jansen, McClurg to thank, that provided the financial support for the magazine. The typography, which remained virtually unchanged for the entire life of the magazine, is clear, straightforward and unadorned, perfectly suited for the "intelligent guide and agreeable companion to the book-lover and book buyer" which the first issue announced its purpose to be.

The first issue also included a column, which was to become a regular feature, "Literary Notes and News," from which we learn that "A new edition of Macauley's complete works, in eight volumes, at the remarkably low price of $10, is announced by Houghton, Osgood & Co." Then there is this bit of news: "Another idol shattered—or badly damaged: Mr. Aldrich, in his new Atlantic story, causes one of his characters—a sailor—to make the scandalous and depressing discovery that Robinson Crusoe's man Friday 'was not a man at all, but a light-minded young princess from one of the neighboring islands who had fallen in love with Robinson,' and that 'her real name was Saturday.' "

When that first issue appeared of Francis Browne's *The Dial*, it must have seemed to him that his life up to that time had been in preparation for this great opportunity. That he was well aware of the cultural, literary and religious ideas of the New England he came from is made clear by his choice of name for his new magazine and the fact that his first issue includes a rather long, detailed and most interesting article, "The Original '*Dial*' " by Norman C. Perkins. The original *Dial*, this article tells us, appeared in Boston as a quarterly from 1840 to 1844 under the editorship of Margaret Fuller, aided by Ralph Waldo Emerson and George Ripley. Mr. Perkins quotes the following from a lecture given some years later by Emerson: "A modest quarterly journal called the 'Dial,' under the editorship of Margaret Fuller, enjoyed its obscurity for four years, when it ended. Its papers were the contributions and work of friendship among a narrow circle of writers. Perhaps its writers were its chief readers. But it had some noble papers; perhaps the

43

best of Margaret Fuller's." Emerson himself was a regular contributor of essays and poetry to that "Dial," as were also, among others, Henry David Thoreau, A. Bronson Alcott and William Ellery Channing. Since Browne was born in 1843, during the time of the "Dial" and the Brook Farm experiment in communal living, it was fitting that this transplanted New Englander should have referred back to that tradition when he launched his literary journal in Chicago.

Having little or no financial resources of his own, it seems doubtful that Browne would have been able to get his magazine off the ground without the participation of Jansen, McClurg & Co., but it must still have been a difficult, discouraging task that required long hours of work and meticulous attention to detail, made all the more difficult by his poor health. According to the obituary written by his son for *The Dial* of June 1, 1913, during the first years of the magazine Browne himself looked after the business details and wrote most of the articles and reviews, in addition to which, to support a large and growing family, he acted as literary advisor to his publisher, which involved, as his son said, "reading and revising book manuscripts, consulting with authors, and coming intimately in contact with those myriad details that go to make up the publishing business." *The Dial* paid its way from the beginning, and however meagre the living it provided for its editor, it soon won a place for itself as a much respected, useful literary journal. That such success did not come easily we can gather from the fact that, according to a doctoral dissertation by Frederic John Mosher on Francis Browne and his associate, William Morton Payne, no less than sixty-seven other literary magazines were launched in Chicago during the first decade of *The Dial*. One of the reasons for the success of Browne's publication, besides the participation of Jansen, McClurg and its consistent high quality, was doubtless its usefulness. To the list of books published during the previous month, arranged by subject, Browne soon added a list of important magazine articles. The two lists must have been particularly useful to librarians and others involved with books at a time when neither service was otherwise available. Francis Browne was an idealist with a missionary zeal for literature and cultural standards, but as the success of his venture makes evident, he also had a firm grasp of reality.

The Dial of July 1892 begins with the announcement, "Messrs. A. C. McClurg & Co. (the name of Jansen, McClurg had been changed a few years before to A. C. McClurg) beg to announce to the friends and readers of *The Dial* that with the present issue their interest in the paper is transferred to Mr. Francis F. Browne, who has been its editor and a part owner since its commencement." After giving the reason for this change—to assure the complete independence of the magazine—the announcement ends with the sentence, "Its successful publication for twelve years, and its already acknowledged position as 'the foremost American critical journal,' will remain a matter of pride to its original publishers, who now part from it with the most hearty good-will and best wishes for its future." The September 1, 1892 issue announced that henceforth *The Dial* would be published twice each month and the subscription price would be raised from $1.50 to $2.00 a year. With that issue the descriptive line at the top of the first page, beneath the title, which from the first issue had been "A Monthly Review and Index of Current Literature" became "A Semi-Monthly Journal of Literary Criticism, Discussion, and Information" and so remained for the rest of its life in Chicago. In this same issue of September 1, 1892, it is interesting to notice, the editor has a word about Chicago. While the place of publication of such a review, he says, "matters very little," he speaks with pride of "the rapid growth of Chicago in other than material directions," and particularly of "its public collection of books," which "are in a fair way to rival those of any other city." His expectations for the future were no doubt influenced by the recent completion of the fine library building on Michigan Avenue between Randolph and Washington streets.

Another displaced New Englander, William Morton Payne, became associated with *The Dial* in 1884, his first contribution a review of the collected poems of Matthew Arnold, which he described as "one of the glories of English literature." During his first years with *The Dial* Payne assumed responsibility for the features "Recent Fiction" and "Recent Poetry," and in 1892 when Browne became sole owner, Payne became literary editor, which he remained until *The Dial* went to New York in 1918. Payne was an exceptionally well-educated man and seems to have been driven by the same missionary zeal for literature which possessed Browne. It is quite appropriate that the title of Mosher's doctoral dissertation on Browne, Payne and *The Dial* is "Chicago's 'Saving Remnant.' " Payne had been brought to Chicago from Massachusetts as a boy by his parents and received a good education—remarkably so, judging from the results—at Chicago's first high school, where courses were offered in Greek, Latin, French, Astronomy, Botany, Chemistry, Rhetoric, History, Geometry, Philosophy, among other subjects, and where he met and became a lifelong friend of Paul Shorey, the first professor of Greek at the University of Chicago. Payne continued his education at the Chicago Public Library under the tutelage of William F. Poole, the librarian, and in 1876, at the age of eighteen, he became a successful and much respected teacher in a Chicago high school. But he gave up teaching when he became associated with *The Dial*. He wrote reviews also for other publications, including two of the Chicago newspapers, and soon established himself, according to Mosher, as "one of the foremost literary critics in America." It was the New England of the founding fathers that produced these two serious, principled men, devoted to learning and determined to bring culture to the prairies.

Francis Browne, as mentioned, had a large family, eventually six sons and three daughters, and he never had an easy time of it financially, whatever esteem and respect he may have won because of his magazine. One of his sons, Francis G. Browne, became business manager in 1894, after Browne became sole owner, and in 1905 another son, Waldo R. Browne became assistant editor and upon the death of his father in 1913, editor. In 1892 Browne set up his own printing shop. This may have been done not only to take advantage of his own knowledge of printing—the appearance of his magazine makes it evident that he had been well trained—but also to make use of the energies of his numerous family.

In the first issue (May 1880) of *The Dial* Browne clearly set forth the critical standards he intended to follow. "Though never hesitating to condemn what is spurious or vicious in literary art, deserved approval will be given with equal readiness and far greater pleasure. . . . While sensible of the obligation to reject the bad and the false, it will be no less mindful of the obligation to conserve the good and true in literature." In the September 1892 issue there appears another statement of its critical standards: "*The Dial* stands preeminently for objective and scientific criticism; it believes in the existence of critical canons, and endeavors to discover and adhere to them." Browne, obviously, was no moral relativist; the difference between good and bad existed and was discoverable. As the magazine became better established, Browne was able to enlist people from all parts of the country to review books for him. Reviews were signed, but because he did not pay his reviewers, he had to rely on nonprofessionals—younger teachers in the universities and colleges, and businessmen and professional people with literary interests. He seems to have had a talent for recognizing promising young writers—among his earlier contributors, for example, were Frederic Jackson Turner, Woodrow Wilson (while still a young professor at Princeton), Norman Foerster, Henry Seidel Canby, Albert Shaw. The following, taken more or less at random, will give some idea of the flavor of *The Dial*:

On Hamlin Garland's *The Eagle's Heart* from the issue of February 16, 1901:

> ... he is the same plain blunt man that he was in 'Main-Travelled Roads,' and has acquired little more of art than he had at the outset of his career. The sense of humor was left out of his composition, and of the finer graces of style his work has remained imperturbably innocent. But he has other qualities, qualities of earnestness and rugged force, that are impressive, ...

On Henry B. Fuller's *The Last Refuge: A Sicilian Romance*, also from the issue of February 16, 1901:

> It must suffice us here to emphasize the charm of Mr. Fuller's manner, and the fact that he has again (as in his first books) produced something that almost deserves the name of a new variety of literary composition.

On Max Beerbohm's *Yet Again* from the issue of March 16, 1910:

Mr. Beerbohm is a bystander, an observer, endowed with the keenest possible sense of the art of life, but amiably detached from all its practical issues. He poses a little; he deliberately cultivates interesting prejudices and significant predispositions. And whatever he chooses to talk about, in a style intimate, elaborate, quite sincere beneath its polish, takes on a new meaning—and keeps it.

Besides signed reviews, news of literary matters and essays on recent fiction and poetry, there were editorials. *The Dial* eschewed politics, but took a strong stand against the Spanish-American War and the annexation of the Philippines, on the grounds that these were not so much political as moral issues. In their general positions, it seems fair to say, Browne·and Payne were old-fashioned, conservative Americans.

The control Browne exercised over his magazine was not autocratic, but rather indirect, by his choice of reviewers. He issued no instructions to reviewers except to "tell us exactly what you think of the book in question." He tried to publish authoritative criticism, but, as was inevitable, it was he, as editor, who decided what was authoritative. In seeking reviewers for fiction, plays or poetry, all he demanded was "sound taste based on established standards." There were many reviews of historical works, and in the early years of the magazine many of these were contributed by William F. Poole, who acted as unofficial historical editor. The Civil War, not surprisingly, was the subject of countless books during those years, and here Browne exercised strict control: he considered the Civil War to have been a holy war, fought to free the slave and save the Union, and anyone who thought differently had no place in his magazine. Poole seems to have felt equally strongly about the New England Puritan tradition, about which he would tolerate no criticism.

By the early 1900s Francis Browne's health had deteriorated to the point where he could no longer face the Chicago winter, and with two sons on the staff of the magazine and William Morton Payne as literary editor, he was able to spend the winters in California, where, as time went on, he spent more and more of the year. He died in California in 1913, at the age of seventy, survived by his wife and all his nine children. Only five years later *The Dial* left Chicago for New York, the issue of June 20, 1918 the last to be published in Chicago. No reason is given for the move; the next issue, that of July 18, 1918 contains only the notice, "*The Dial* is now established in its New York office, at 152 West Thirteenth Street, to which all communications should hereafter be addressed. . . . Beginning October 3 publication will be weekly." The death of Francis Browne, his son remarked, " . . . occasioned little comment outside the circle of those who in one way or another came in direct contact with his personality," and no doubt the transfer to New York of the magazine that was his life work and had made a great contribution to the cultural life of the city was not the occasion for much comment either—Chicago, then as now, was far more concerned with other affairs. It has even been said that while people from Chicago were inclined to boast about the fact that the most distinguished literary magazine in the country was published in their city, the publication had far more subscribers in New York than in Chicago. In any case, by the time *The Dial* went to New York, that city had become the center of publishing and literary life and it is certain also that Waldo Browne possessed neither the determination of his father nor the single-minded dedication that had driven him to overcome whatever obstacle lay in his path.

Perhaps the most important reason for the change of ownership and editorial direction was the fact that the literary and critical standards represented by the old *Dial* were changing. In this connection it is significant that Waldo Browne was outraged by T. S. Eliot's amusing little poem, *Cousin Nancy*, which was published in 1917 in a collection, *Prufrock and Other Observations*— *Prufrock* itself having first been published, at the instigation of Ezra Pound, in Harriet Monroe's *Poetry*. *Cousin Nancy* contains only thirteen lines; these are the last seven:

> *Miss Nancy Ellicott smoked*
> *And danced all the modern dances;*
> *And her aunts were not quite sure how they felt about it,*
> *But they knew that it was modern.*

Upon the glazen shelves kept watch
Matthew and Waldo, guardians of the faith,
The army of unalterable law.

One can see why Waldo Browne might have been incensed.

After its move to New York, however, *The Dial* in 1921 and 1922 published Eliot's *London Letters*, and in November 1922, one month after it came out in London, the first American edition of *The Waste Land*. The seemingly stable world represented by Francis Browne, William Morton Payne and *The Dial*, the world of Emerson, Brook Farm, Matthew Arnold and Tennyson, had ended with the bloody, senseless battles of the First World War. "The antagonist world," as Russell Kirk puts it in his book *Eliot and His Age*, "was at hand; but so was the Age of Eliot, with its resignation, its penitence, its defense of permanent things, and its stubborn hope." If Waldo Browne was outraged by Eliot's whimsical *Cousin Nancy*, it seems doubtful that he would have known what to do with *The Waste Land*. *The Dial* of Francis Browne had been a constructive influence and served an important purpose, but the times, it seems, had passed it by.

It is worth mentioning that Eliot was not overly impressed with the new *Dial*: in a letter to John Quinn in 1920, he remarked that it was an exact copy of the dull *Atlantic Monthly* and went on to say, "There is far too much in it, and it is all second-rate and exceedingly solemn." He may have thought differently, of course, after *The Dial* published *The Waste Land*. In any case, *The Dial* survived in New York only until 1929.

In writing of his father, Waldo Browne described "the predominant notes of his character" as "simplicity, sincerity, courage, persistency." He was a quiet, unassuming man, much beloved by his friends and associates, demanded much of himself, was unswerving in pursuing the goals he believed in, and had a strong sense of justice. When the American press was hounding Governor Altgeld for having pardoned the "anarchists" who had been accused, and wrongfully so, as it was later proved, of throwing the bomb at the time of the Haymarket Riot, Francis Browne prepared a detailed vindication for an English publication, and in the emotional orgy that led to the disgraceful war with Spain, Browne kept his head and didn't hesitate to express his views, as he did again at the time of the annexation of the Philippines. Browne was never given much recognition by Chicago for his contribution to its cultural life, nor, for that matter, much support. He always had to labor, not only against ill-health and poverty, but as his son put it, "More powerfully deterrent than all these combined was the spirit of the time and the place of his labors—the all-pervading materialism to which intellectual concerns were chiefly clap-trap and high purposes moonshine." An uncle of Francis Browne, like him of solidly Puritan inheritance, went to Japan as a missionary where he made the first translation of the New Testament into Japanese, which he himself set into type and printed on his own press. When Francis Browne came in 1867 to bring culture to the muddy, brawling city on the shore of Lake Michigan, he was doubtless impelled by the same spirit that sent his uncle to bring Christianity to the heathen.

As noted earlier, Francis Browne was the founder of the Chicago Literary Club. At the time he was struggling to keep his *Lakeside Monthly* alive, shortly after having recovered from two disastrous fires and the panic of 1873, he was laid low by illness. He was forced to leave the city, not to return until 1880, and not being able to attend a meeting of the Club he had founded, was expelled for nonpayment of dues, which hurt him deeply. It was not until 1899 that the Club realized its error and made him an honorary member, but it was too late for him to take an active part. It would seem, therefore, that the Club was not much more appreciative of Browne's efforts to bring literary culture to the prairies than was the rest of Chicago. In connection with all this, it is worth mentioning also that Browne refused to join the Cliff Dwellers Club founded in 1908 by Hamlin Garland—he thought it lacking in moral dignity and high seriousness.

It was a great achievement to found a literary magazine in Chicago in 1880 and to keep it going for almost thirty-five years without compromising its standards. Its founder and editor for all those years not only made a significant contribution to Chicago and the Middle West by encouraging authors and creating an atmosphere favorable to literary production, but by its high standards of criticism it must also have had a constructive influence on literature in general. The quality of writing at any time is influenced, for better or for worse, by the level of criticism; whether they like it or not, writers are influenced by what critics have to say, as are publishers as well. It is unfortunate that Chicago does not now have such a literary magazine as *The Dial* was in its great days, which would review books on the basis of what they said and how well they said it rather than in accordance with the ideological whims of the reviewer. It may well be that the country is at such a turning point in matters of spirit as that which Eliot's *The Waste Land* marked so sharply. It also seems evident that New York is losing some of its dominance of literary life—of publishing, of criticism and all that goes with it—in which case the time may have come for Chicago to reassert itself, for a magazine with the aspirations and high standards of the old *Dial* to appear again in Chicago.

Harper:
The Providential Man

A DEFINING STEP in a community's progress to cultural eminence is the founding of a university. Higher education—the passing on of civilization from one generation to the next—can mark a city with greatness. In this Chicago was most fortunate. As the city prepared for the twentieth century, it could do so with pride for it possessed a remarkable university, founded by a remarkable man.

When the present University of Chicago opened its doors to students on October 1, 1892 with William Rainey Harper as president and with the financial backing of John D. Rockefeller, it was positioned to take its place as one of the great universities of the country as, in fact, it soon did, becoming as well a cultural triumph for Chicago. Although workmen were still finishing its Gothic

William Rainey Harper

buildings with professors and students finding their way among the debris and confusion of construction, a distinguished faculty of one hundred and twenty was already in place, prepared to carry out the mandate of President Harper, who made it clear that the new institution was not to be another traditional American college, but a *university*, the purpose of which was "... not to stock the student's mind with knowledge of what had already been accomplished in a given field, but rather so to train him that he himself may be able to push out along new lines of investigation."

The present university is not the first University of Chicago, but the result of a development that began in 1856 with the founding of a much more modest institution, which came about through the offer of ten acres of land by Senator Stephen A. Douglas. After being declined by the Presbyterians, his gift was accepted by the Baptists, who agreed to raise the $100,000 the donor made as a condition of his donation for the building that was to be erected on the site. This was at a time when, with a population of less than 90,000, Chicago was rather a large frontier town than a city. It says much for the idealism and faith of those Chicago Baptists that they were willing to undertake the founding of a university at a time when the energies of its citizens were necessarily largely devoted to raising a city out of the swamp at the mouth of the Chicago River and the surrounding prairie.

A substantial building was dedicated in 1859 and a law school opened the same year. The first catalog was issued in 1860 when the university had a total enrollment of 178, which grew steadily in subsequent years. The majority of the twenty trustees were Baptists, the charter stipulating that the president and a majority of the board "shall forever be of the same religious denomination as the majority of this corporation," but any sort of religious test or requirement for election to a teaching position or admission to the university was excluded. The university was to "be open alike to persons of any religious faith or profession," but was recognized as a Christian, but not sectarian, institution.

The times were not kind to the aspirations of the founders. Following the panic of 1857 when the pledges for the first $100,000 fund drive, which was to pay for the building, remained largely unfulfilled, came the Civil War, then the Great Fire of 1871, the Panic of 1873 and the less devastating fire of 1874. Almost from its beginning, the university was plagued by debt and inadequate financing, and in spite of a loyal constituency, educational work was discontinued in 1886. In the meantime, however, a seminary for the study of theology had been established in 1867 as a part of the university, which in 1877 became a separate institution, under the sponsorship of the Baptist Theological Union, and moved to Morgan Park, south of Chicago. John D. Rockefeller became a generous supporter of the seminary and for nine years served as vice-president of the Baptist Theological Union. Equally crucial for the founding of the present University of Chicago was the calling of William Rainey Harper on January 1, 1879 to the chair of Hebrew at the Morgan Park seminary. Harper was twenty-two years old at the time, having received his doctorate three years earlier from Yale. It was the Baptist seminary in Morgan Park, therefore, that brought the two men together who were largely responsible for the founding of the present University of Chicago.

The nineteenth century in America was a time when faith in education as the basis for an orderly society reigned supreme, as is evidenced by the public school movement, the Northwest Ordinance, the colleges, many of them of denominational origin, which dot the countryside, and the first state universities. It is not surprising, therefore, that the leaders of the Baptist Church looked upon the failure of the first University of Chicago as a challenge to establish a major university under Baptist auspices and in Chicago, not only because Chicago was the site of their earlier failure, but perhaps principally because Chicago seemed, more than any other city, to represent the dynamism and confidence of contemporary America.

Another key figure in all this was Thomas W. Goodspeed, who was then secretary of the Baptist seminary in Morgan Park. It was he who wrote the first letter to Mr. Rockefeller proposing the establishment of a new university in Chicago. This was at the time when Dr. Harper had declined the offer of the presidency of the old university, which was on its last legs, and was considering an attractive offer from Yale. Of particular interest in all this are

Goodspeed's comments about Harper, whom he obviously had in mind as president of the university he was proposing to Mr. Rockefeller:

> The circumstances seem to us to point to Dr. Harper as the providential man. Yale is pressing him for a decisive answer. They have just written urging him to accept within 20 days. . . . We know that he has all the qualifications to lead in this undertaking, immense capacity for work, great abilities as a scholar, boundless courage, eminent gifts as an organizer and administrator, fitness for reaching men and securing their confidence and help, and that he is a born teacher, who can call students about him and command their love and admiration and get all the work out of them of which they are capable.

This letter, which put the series of events in motion that culminated with the opening of the University on October 1, 1892 is quoted in full in Goodspeed's history of the institution, but no date is indicated. It must have been written in early 1886, because a brief reply from Mr. Rockefeller follows dated April 13, 1886. In any case, this exchange of letters was followed by the organization in 1887 of the American Baptist Education Society which served as the focal point of the various groups interested in founding the University and for the depositing of contributions. From then on, events moved rapidly. The annual meeting of the Education Society in 1889 was held in Boston. Resolutions were adopted committing the Society to "the founding of a well-equipped College in the City of Chicago," and providing that "the privileges of the institution be extended to persons of both sexes on equal terms," and "that the Board proceed to raise one million dollars as a financial foundation for the proposed institution." It was further resolved "that the President of the institution and two-thirds of the Board of Trustees of the same shall always be members of Baptist churches." It was at this meeting that Frederick T. Gates, the Corresponding Secretary of the Society, read a letter from Mr. Rockefeller committing himself to contribute $600,000 for the establishment of the proposed institution, provided $400,000 more were pledged by June 1, 1890. This announcement was greeted with prolonged applause and the singing by the entire assembly of the doxology, *Praise God from Whom all blessings flow.*

To raise $400,000 at a time when it cost two cents to mail a letter was a formidable undertaking, which Dr. Goodspeed in his history describes as follows:

> There was no hesitation as to where the first appeal must be made, or from whom the larger part of the money to be raised must come. The new institution was to be located in Chicago. It was to be founded under Baptist auspices. It was to be, as far as possible, the contribution of the denomination to the cause of education. It was to reestablish in Chicago that educational work the failure of which had been a sorrow and humiliation. The chief appeal must be to the Baptists of Chicago. They were a comparatively feeble folk financially. But they understood perfectly that the responsibility for the success of the campaign rested, in the first instance, on them.

On May 23, 1890, the designated officers of the Baptist Education Society notified Mr. Rockefeller by telegram that the condition of his grant, that they raise an additional $400,000, had been fulfilled. Of this amount, according to the Goodspeed history, $233,000 had come from the Baptists of Chicago, $116,000 from Baptists outside Chicago, $27,000 from Jewish groups in Chicago, most of it from members of the Standard Club, and $30,000 from alumni of the old university. Marshall Field I gave ten acres of land in The Midway Plaisance and an option to purchase an additional ten acres for $132,500, which became the site of the new university. The report of the Executive Board to the American Baptist Educational Society at its annual meeting in Chicago on May 27 and 28, 1890, concludes:

> The new University is to be a Christian institution. It is to be forever under the auspices of the Baptist denomination. It is to be conducted in a spirit of the widest liberality, seeking thus to deserve the sympathy and cooperation of all public-spirited men, and inviting to its halls the largest possible number of students from

57

every class of the community that it may give to them a true
Christian culture.

The foregoing makes clear that the founders of the University of
Chicago were Baptists and that the one million dollars that
launched the University came largely from members of Baptist
churches. Furthermore, that it was their intention that the University be a Christian institution and remain under the auspices of the
Baptist denomination. But whatever the intentions of the founders
may have been, and the goodwill of those who followed them in
administering the University to honor the wishes of the founders, it
hardly seems possible that a university established in the tradition of
the nineteenth-century German university, as the University of Chicago was, dedicated to *Lehre und Forschung*, that is, to teaching
and investigation, could long remain under the control of a religious
denomination. In this connection, it is instructive to observe that
when Robert M. Hutchins, who was then a communicant of the
Presbyterian church, was called in 1929 to the presidency of the
University, the requirement that the president and a majority of
the board be Baptists had long since been dropped, but Harold
Swift, who was then Chairman of the Board, is quoted to have said
at the time, "Our president has always been a member of a Protestant church, which we consider very desirable in view of the fact
that it is the purpose of the board to insure the continuance of the
University forever as a Christian institution." Forever, it hardly
seems necessary to add, is a long time.

All this notwithstanding, the founding and fostering of an institution that was to become a university, acclaimed not only for its
instruction but for its research and for its expansion of knowledge
and culture, was an accomplishment that casts much glory on
Chicago which, for all its getting and spending, managed somehow
to surmount its limitations, a truly exceptional achievement.

Hutchins:
The Worthy Successor*

ROBERT M. HUTCHINS, from his becoming president of the University of Chicago in 1929 at the age of thirty to his resignation in 1951, if not the most influential head of a university during those years, was certainly the most prominent.

The appointment of the young Hutchins to the presidency of the University of Chicago was a media event of major proportions, made all the more so by the striking appearance of a tall, handsome man and his attractive, fashionably dressed young wife. As happy a choice as it seemed to be, and as consistent with the tradition for innovation established by William Rainey Harper, who was thirty-five when in 1891 with Rockefeller money he launched the university, it was not made without considerable self-questioning on the part of the trustees. The obvious choice seemed to be Frederick Woodward, the vice president who had acted as president following the resignation of Max Mason in the spring of 1928, but several influential members of the faculty objected strongly on the grounds that Woodward would emphasize the college at the expense of a university committed to research they felt the proper mission of the University of Chicago to be. Hutchins, as it happened, was not even included among the fifty-six names the faculty search committee had compiled, which is not surprising, for although he had been made secretary of the Yale Corporation at the age of twenty-seven, during which time he finished his studies at the Law School, and was made Dean of the Law School two years later, he was better known as the "boy wonder" of Yale than as an academic administrator. When Hutchins was first proposed, after meeting five of the trustees at a luncheon arranged by Woodward, some doubt was expressed

---

* From a review of *Unseasonable Truths: The Life of Robert Maynard Hutchins*, by Harry S. Ashmore, Boston: Little, Brown, 1989, which was published in the quarterly *Modern Age*, Fall, 1990.

Robert Maynard Hutchins

because of his age and inexperience, which was not lessened by a letter from President James R. Angell of Yale, which ended with this paragraph:

> If he develops as he now promises, he should in five or ten years be an extraordinarily able and well trained man. I cannot believe that at present he is mature enough wisely to shoulder so grave and critically important a task as that of your presidency.

The carefully written letter from President Angell, who, having been a dean of the University of Chicago, was in a position to know the challenges Hutchins would face, and, having made him secretary of the Yale Corporation, also to judge his ability to meet them, may well have settled the issue, had not Harold Swift, a longtime member of the board, a generous supporter of the university, and at this time the Chairman, taken a strong position in his favor. After having made a careful investigation of his own, Swift reported to the board, "There is no doubt this man is an administrator," and in reply to President Angell's doubts about Hutchins' youth and inexperience, he suggested that the president of Yale may well have been influenced by his desire to keep such a promising young man for his own university. Whatever hesitation there may have been on the part of the trustees, Chairman Swift carried them all before him, and on April 26, 1929, with the unanimous approval of the board, it was announced that Robert M. Hutchins had been chosen to become the President of the University of Chicago.

The photograph of the smiling, self-assured young Hutchins with his attractive wife arriving in a Chicago railroad station to assume his duties as president of the university is somehow reminiscent of F. Scott Fitzgerald and his wife Zelda, which raises the question whether the trustees in their choice of the thirty-year-old Hutchins may not unwittingly have reflected the infatuation with youth and the confidence in the future that marked the 1920s. When Hutchins was elected president of the university in April 1929, the stock market crash that marked the beginning of the Great Depression was only six months in the future, but when he was inaugurated with appropriate academic formality in the new Rockefeller Chapel on November 12, 1929, the depression had clearly begun.

The new president was an extraordinarily talented man as his career had already demonstrated. An effective speaker, he could memorize a speech after reading it three times and always spoke without text or notes; had developed a fine, clear, spare literary style; was a speed reader who assimilated what he read; had a quick wit, a photographic memory, gracious manners. All of this, combined with great energy and self-confidence, made him a formidable personality. He is often compared with his predecessor, William Rainey Harper, but there was a great difference. When Harper, at the age of thirty-five, founded the university and became its president, he was a distinguished and much respected scholar and teacher, whereas Hutchins, a brilliant student first at Oberlin, where he completed two years, after which he graduated from Yale with high honors, could make no claim to scholarly distinction, nor except for two years of teaching at a preparatory school and a few courses in the Yale Law School, to experience in teaching. On this subject, his biographer Harry S. Ashmore has the following to say:

> Upon his precipitate elevation to the rank of university president, Robert Hutchins took stock of his own learning and recognized that he had arrived at the age of thirty with "some knowledge of the Bible, of Shakespeare, of *Faust*, of one dialogue of Plato, and of the opinions of many semi-literate and a few literate judges, and that was about all."

While Hutchins' education was by no means as deficient as he represented it—self-depreciation was almost a rhetorical device with him—he was determined to use his position as head of an influential university to make sure that future generations of students would fare better than he had, which led to his first confrontation with his faculty. While still Dean of the Yale Law School he had met Mortimer Adler, who, as a participant in the Great Books program instituted by John Erskine at Columbia University, had become a zealous advocate and converted Hutchins to the cause of the Great Books as the most effective road to a broad education. Soon after his appointment as president, but before his formal inauguration, Hutchins invited Adler to join him in Chicago, and at the latter's suggestion, the new President recommended that Adler,

Richard McKeon of Columbia, and Scott Buchanan of the University of Virginia be asked to join the philosophy faculty—the latter two having been associated with Adler in the Great Books program at Columbia. The faculty finally accepted McKeon, but distrusted Buchanan, who later went to St. John's, and rejected Adler, who eventually taught in the Law School. Before it was all over, three distinguished members of the faculty resigned in protest at the manner in which the appointments had been made, or rather attempted. Adler, however, remained closely associated with Hutchins to the very end, and at the university was regarded as his philosophical mentor. Ashmore describes the end of the episode as follows:

> As he turned his attention to these matters, the young president
> recognized that he really had no clear idea of what a sound educa-
> tion ought to be. At this point, he later said, his own education
> began—under the tutelage of the redoubtable Mortimer Adler.

Hutchins was more successful with a proposal to restructure the university in accordance with a plan which had been worked out in a general way during the administration of Max Mason. This plan provided for placing the academic departments into four divisions: humanities, social sciences, physical sciences, and biological sciences; and establishing the College as an independent fifth division, each to be headed by a dean who would be responsible to the president. This plan had been approved by a number of key members of the faculty, and was accepted by the University Senate and the Board of Trustees. Establishing the College as a separate division gave Hutchins the opportunity to fulfill his desire to raise the standard of undergraduate education by giving it a more coherent structure and definite purpose, a cause to which he devoted much of his time and energy during the next fifteen years. Hutchins' conception of education and his determination to use his position as the head of a great university to give American education a degree of organization and purpose he felt it did not have, can be gained from Hutchins' numerous speeches on the subject and his several books.

The plan which Hutchins proposed for the restructuring of the College, he never tired of repeating, was only carrying out Harper's original scheme: Students who demonstrated their qualification by examination would be admitted to the College after two years of high school, and after finishing four years of college would be granted the bachelor's degree and be ready for specialized training in the graduate school. In innumerable articles and speeches, Hutchins argued that the traditional eight years of grade school and four years of high school, followed by four years of college, unnecessarily prolonged adolescence, were fragmentary and unstructured, and did not provide the student with the broad, general education he needed, whether he intended to go on to graduate school or to end his formal education.

The following from a speech, "The Sheep Look Up," given in 1935, and included in his book *No Friendly Voice* (1936), describes the general education that the college he had in mind would offer:

> A program of general education which is based on ideas, which leads the student to understand the nature and schemes of history, to grasp the principles of science, to comprehend the fine arts and literature, and to which philosophy contributes intelligibility at every stage, is the kind of program that we must now construct.

Hutchins was able to win the approval of the trustees for his "Chicago Plan" for the College, as it came to be called, but was never able to gain the wholehearted support of the faculty. To work out the course of study which would offer the general education that was an integral part of the plan, he asked Richard McKeon, who had become Dean of the Humanities Division, to head a Committee on Liberal Arts that would assume this responsibility. Hutchins, to assure the independence of the committee, obtained anonymous gifts to fund it for three years, and McKeon, as chairman, was joined by Mortimer Adler and Scott Buchanan. The committee immediately ran into opposition from the faculty, at least partly, without doubt, because of the presence of Adler, and worse still, the members began to disagree among themselves: The Great Books idea they accepted, but should their study begin with Aristotle or Aquinas? By the end of the year the committee was dissolved and Buchanan invited to become dean and head of instruction at St. John's College in Annapolis. Hutchins' "Chicago Plan" was logical and could have provided a model for the much-needed restructuring of American education. During the short time the new plan was tried at the University of Chicago it was shown that it made good sense and turned out outstanding students, but the graduate schools of the University would not accept the products of the plan without further study, and the collapse of the Committee on the Liberal Arts meant that the new curriculum needed to carry out its mandate "to do the work of the University in general education" was never fully worked out. In spite of Hutchins' eloquent plea for order and structure in education, for what he called general education, the country's public schools continued to suffer, and still suffer, as is agreed on all sides, from mediocrity and aimlessness. The sheep, as Hutchins put it, are still not being fed.

Robert Hutchins, as he often remarked, was a child of the parsonage. When he was born, his father was a successful and much respected minister in a Presbyterian church in Brooklyn. He was called to Oberlin College in Ohio to become a professor in the seminary when his son Robert was eight. Oberlin since its founding in the 1830s had been devoted to social improvement, or, in current terminology, to the social gospel. Artemus Ward, who visited Oberlin during the Civil War, spoke of the college as "A grate place where the day begins with prayer, followed by a reading from the *New York Tribune*." Hutchins described his growing up in Oberlin, where he stayed through the first two years of college, as "life on a Puritan island," but in spite of his strict Calvinist background and the austerity of the parsonage, he had no difficulty accepting the style of life provided by the University and its Chairman, Harold Swift.

"Although he would continue to profess a puritanical disdain for material goods," his biographer writes, "Hutchins had no difficulty in adapting to the rarefied surroundings those with unlimited means could provide for themselves and their chosen companions. He might have justified this indulgence as a necessary part of his job. Instead, in his usual sardonic fashion, he described his attitude as that of the man who said he had no desire to become a millionaire—he just wanted to live like one."

The presidential residence was a substantial establishment, well equipped for entertaining, and supplied with five live-in servants, a full-time gardener and a chauffeur for the limousine supplied by the university—a very different style of life from that of a Presbyterian parsonage. Hutchins readily adjusted himself to it, and, as his later life demonstrated, quite obviously became rather dependent on it.

Hutchins was still a communicant in the Presbyterian church when he came to Chicago and regularly attended the services in Rockefeller Chapel until one Sunday, his biographer relates, "the Reverend Charles Whitney Gilkey opened his sermon, 'Yesterday I was on the golf course, and as I teed off, I was reminded that we must follow through in life.' " Hutchins is reported as once saying of this incident:

> If you are the son and grandson of ministers and have had to go to church twice on Sunday, to Sunday School and to the Wednesday-evening meeting of the Young People's Society for Christian Endeavor, you are entitled to be spared from the continuation of such formalities when you have anything serious to do. Because these were not serious gatherings. They were social assemblies of one kind or another. And my objection to the truths that were delivered by Mr. Gilkey was not that they were untrue, but that I had heard them over and over again. And frequently or sometimes in a better literary framework.

"The good habits of his youth," his biographer Ashmore goes on to say, "survived the rejection of the faith of his fathers. Hutchins was never to shirk the obligations of any office he held or those he imposed upon himself as a matter of conscience. He continued to act upon his belief that it was possible to maintain 'those habits of mind and conduct which are generally defined as Christian without having faith in one God, the Creator, or having faith in the immortality of the soul or any of the other central doctrines of religion.' " Hutchins, in an article, "The Administrator," which appeared in the *Journal of Higher Education* in 1946, speaks of courage, fortitude, justice and prudence as the "minimum qualifications of an administrator." Although the administrator needs the theological virtues of faith, hope and charity more than most men, he omitted them, he went on to say, "because they come through divine grace, and I am talking about what the administrator can accomplish by his own efforts."

In connection with all this it is interesting, and perhaps revealing of Hutchins' view of the world, that in his farewell address, following his resignation from the university, "A Message to the Young Generation" (reprinted in *Measure*, Fall 1951), he told students:

> The whole doctrine that we must adjust ourselves to our environment, which I take to be the prevailing doctrine of American education, seems to me radically erroneous. Our mission here on earth is to change our environment, not to adjust ourselves to it. If we become maladjusted in the process, so much the worse for the environment. If we have to choose between Sancho Panza and Don Quixote, let us by all means choose Don Quixote.

Because Hutchins does not define what he means by environment, nor how far he thinks we can or should go in changing it, it is impossible to know what he really meant with his advice to the young generation. Among the virtues Hutchins prescribed for the administrator, he did not include humility.

William Morgenstern, who as director of public relations for the University was closely associated with Hutchins for many years, said that Hutchins one day remarked that no university president should remain in office for more than ten years, that this would give him time to put any original ideas he may have had into effect, and that by then he would have made so many enemies that further influence would be impossible. Richard McKeon confirmed that Hutchins had said the same to him. Why, then, did he stay for more than twenty years? Adler, according to Ashmore, after their failure to restructure the college in the way they both wanted, urged Hutchins to consider going to St. John's as president, where he would have been welcomed, but after a visit to the college, which included his wife's firm notice that she had no intention of moving to Annapolis, Hutchins sent the following note to Adler:

There is no answer to it. What you say about Chicago is true. What is the alternative? I don't want to go to Saint John's. There isn't any other place I can go. I have thought and thought but I can think of no alternative. I could resign without an alternative. That hardly seems the act of a prudent man.

Hutchins seems to have made no effort to obtain another academic appointment nor, apparently, was one offered to him, but he did attempt to win an appointment to the Supreme Court. He enlisted the support of such influential members of the Roosevelt administration as Harold Ickes and Thomas Corcoran, both of whom he regarded as friends, and William O. Douglas who, in a letter to Hutchins, referred to himself as Hutchins' "agent" in the matter. But as it finally worked out, it was Douglas who was appointed in 1939 to the seat left vacant by the death of Justice Louis Brandeis. When T. V. Smith, the University of Chicago professor who had become a congressman, asked Thomas Corcoran what had happened to the Hutchins appointment, Corcoran supposedly said, "The truth was . . . that the 'Boss' was not certain that Hutchins was on 'our' side." Morgenstern remarked that Hutchins once considered running for governor of Illinois, but then decided against it for the reason that he would be constitutionally unable to make the compromises that would be necessary to win an election. When one considers that two recent governors of Illinois have gone to jail, it seems a great reflection on the political system that a man of Hutchins' superb talents and rich experience would not even consider himself as a candidate because of his unwillingness to compromise.

His Oberlin and Yale backgrounds doubtlessly inclined Hutchins to a liberal point of view; in a speech to the Young Democrats Club, for example, he referred to the Republican Party as the "party of special privileges," the party of "false conservatism," and recommended that "steps be taken to eliminate private profit from banking," positions that were clearly influenced by the fact that the speech was made at the 1932 Democratic convention, but as his strong opposition to "progressive" education and to the European War in 1940 demonstrated, he was not a doctrinaire liberal.

Hutchins was above all a man of principle, which was no doubt the reason that President Roosevelt, with his unerring political judgment, did not feel him to be "on our side."

In his book *The Higher Learning in America* (1936), Hutchins makes a rather categorical statement: "If education is rightly understood, it will be understood as the cultivation of the intellect." With such a view of education it is not surprising that he would not have regarded intercollegiate football as appropriate for a university, and in 1940 at his recommendation and with the approval of the trustees, it was summarily abolished. No other innovation of Hutchins attracted the attention of the press as did this one and to this day it remains the single most publicized event in Hutchins' career. Professor McKeon has said that Hutchins more than once remarked to him that when he came to Chicago one of his principal objectives was to make the University a great center for learning, but, he would add, it ended with the Fermi Institute and the atomic bomb. All of which makes it the more ironical that the first successful fission of the atom, the necessary first step to the bomb, took place in the laboratory that had been set up for the purpose in the abandoned football stadium, Stagg Field. The atomic bomb, however, was not so much a triumph of the University of Chicago, if triumph is the proper word, as of American society—Dwight Macdonald in his magazine *Politics* remarked at the time of Hiroshima that the atomic bomb was as American as the electric refrigerator.

With his quick wit and keen intelligence—not to forget the influence of Yale of the 1920s—Hutchins had an irresistible urge to wisecrack, which gave an impression of flippancy, but nothing shows his intense seriousness more strikingly than his attitude toward World War II and his realistic prediction of its consequences, which is evident from the following from Hutchins' letter to a close friend and confidant, John U. Nef, who was Chairman of the Committee on Social Thought at the University; the letter was written in September 1939, just a few days after the outbreak of war:

> The war has got me down. I wish I could think that it will be short or that we could stay out of it. I think it will be long, and that though we should stay out of it, we are not likely to. I remember

1914 with horror and 1917 with something worse. I don't see either that, after the war is over, though Hitler will be gone, the actions of the French and English governments will be any more enlightened than they were after the last war.

At the end of the war, Hutchins gave two great speeches at University convocations, one to mark the end of the war with Germany, and the other to mark the end of the war with Japan, which are both on the high level of Lincoln's "With malice toward none" speech. As his biographer, Ashmore, says, "It is difficult to imagine any other university president, then or now, delivering a public address comparable to the one he made on 'The New Realism' at a University convocation while the country was still celebrating the victory over Nazi Germany." This speech begins, "The words *peace, justice, cooperation, community,* and *charity* have fallen out of our vocabulary." With his customary eloquence and clarity, Hutchins pleaded not only for justice and charity, but also for intelligence and clear-headedness in facing the problems the war had left behind. If ever Hutchins rose to the true greatness that was in him, it was on the occasion of these two speeches.

It is evident from the letter Hutchins had sent to Mortimer Adler following their visit to St. John's in 1938 that he didn't necessarily feel committed to Chicago for the rest of his life, but as he said in that letter, "What was the alternative?" Where was he to go that would provide the income he needed to maintain the style of life he had been accustomed to and that would give him the platform to promote the causes he felt it his duty to further? The Ford Foundation, which through the death of Edsel Ford had suddenly become the largest foundation in the country, seemed to provide the answer: On December 19, 1950, Hutchins accepted the position of associate director with Paul Hoffman, who was a friend and had been a trustee of the University. On the same day he informed the University Council that he was resigning as Chancellor—a title he had assumed in 1945—to take effect June 30, 1951. Hutchins by then was only fifty-one and still a vigorous man, but, as McKeon commented, among heads of major universities, after more than twenty-one years, he was almost a Rip van Winkle. During the six years since the ending of the war, not only had he brought the University back to its original purpose from an institution that had been for more than three years little more than a subsidiary of the Pentagon, but he also had acted as chairman of the Commission on Freedom of the Press, which his friend Henry Luce had financed with a $200,000 grant. The book that published the findings of that Commission, *A Free and Responsible Press*, with emphasis on "responsible," still makes a critical comment on the media, which typical of Hutchins' insight, seems even more relevant today. Hutchins had also served as chairman of the Committee to Frame a World Constitution (which he privately referred to as the Committee to Frame Hutchins), of the Goethe Bicentennial Celebration in 1949, and of the editorial committee of the quarterly *Measure* (for which he supplied the name).

Hutchins' association with the Ford Foundation did not prove to be as serene as he may well have expected. To be sure, he did not have a recalcitrant faculty to deal with nor (with the income of one-half billion dollars to distribute) any need to raise money, which had been a never-ending task in Chicago. But as had been the case at the University, his increasing predilection for taking unpopular positions, often for no other apparent reason than to demonstrate his independence, caused problems with the trustees. By the time he had given away $89 million of Ford money for various educational projects, which was his field of interest, including $640,000 for Mortimer Adler's Institute for Philosophical Research and $826,000 for the Great Books Foundation, the time seemed to have come for the parting of the ways.

A separate tax-exempt organization, the Fund for the Republic, was established with $15 million of Ford money, Paul Hoffman was made president and Hutchins vice-president, and both resigned from the Foundation. The usual embarrassing situation soon developed in connection with the new Fund—Hutchins made a public statement that "he wouldn't hesitate to hire a Communist for a job he was qualified to do provided I was in a position to see he did it," and it was disclosed that Earl Browder, the head of the Communist Party in the United States, had been hired as a consultant in connection with a study the Fund had sponsored to study Communist infiltration of American institutions. Several trustees resigned, and by a process which, in the rather confusing account of all these developments, never became quite clear, the Great Issues program sponsored by Hutchins for the Fund eventually became the Center for Democratic Institutions, which was located in a mansion overlooking the Pacific in Santa Barbara, California and to which Hutchins gave the name El Parthenon.

The Center for the Study of Democratic Institutions was to be a community of scholars who would discuss the great issues of the day, and, it was hoped, come to helpful conclusions. Hutchins had said many times, beginning when he was Dean of the Yale Law School, that the "ideal intellectual institution is an intellectual community." Hutchins is quoted as reporting to the board of the Center in 1976:

> ... The Center has been able to carry out its mission of identifying and clarifying the basic issues and widening the circles of discussion about them. The constitutional questions raised by the Campaign Practices Act and the revision of the federal criminal code; the moral and legal problems inherent in the effort to provide decent housing for all our people and at the same time preserve the environment; the necessity of innovation in world organization to meet threats to survival; new issues concerning the freedom and responsibility of the press; the possibilities of liberal education in the United States; full employment; planning; equality—these are among the topics being debated in Santa Barbara.

Besides the daily gatherings of the "Fellows" of the Center, who were also joined by invited guests, such subjects as those mentioned above were discussed and, it was expected, clarified. The Center sponsored three great international convocations, *Pacem in Terris*, the first in New York in 1965. It opened in the assembly hall of the United Nations with a speech by Vice President Hubert Humphrey, which was followed by three days of speeches, dinners, and the inevitable panel discussion in the New York Hilton Hotel. John Jessup described it in *Life* magazine as "An extraordinary gathering of the world's movers and shakers . . . to grapple with a staggeringly ambitious project: solutions to the eternal problems of war." How much these three well-publicized gatherings of "movers and shakers" actually accomplished is hard to say, but it seems clear that those stalward Poles, of whom such men as Lech Walesa and the murdered priest Popieluszko are striking examples, motivated as they were by unshakable faith, did more for peace by challenging Communism than those intellectuals discussing the great issues of the day in a New York hotel.

Hutchins had great hopes for the Center. In a letter to Thornton Wilder in 1966 he spoke of it as the "model university of the future," but two years after his death on May 14, 1977, the directors let go the last of its employees and turned over its remaining assets to the University of California in Santa Barbara. The last years of Hutchins' life, from his resignation from the University in 1951 to his death in 1977, are thoroughly depressing. It seems such a waste, a waste of talent, time, resources, opportunities, and what, in the end, did it accomplish? There was an air of unreality about the whole operation: for example, Elizabeth Borgese's dog, which she was trying to teach to pick out letters on an oversized typewriter; that relic of the New Deal, Rexford Guy Tugwell, working out a model constitution; and the slightly decayed California mansion that housed the Center.

It seems such a sad ending to a great career. It is better to recall Hutchins in his great days, when, in one of his wonderfully clear, eloquent speeches in defense of seriousness in education, he offered "the dazzling prospect of millions of young Americans receiving an education adapted to their needs at the hands of teachers who are educated themselves," and proposed the means to bring it about, or when, as president, he made the University of Chicago an exciting place and a great center of intellectual life. Of course Hutchins did have his blind spots: his faith in the Great Books and the Socratic dialogue as the solution of the world's ills; his ignorance of the people who make up the productive part of society, of those who produce the goods and bring them to market, which made it impossible for him to understand the deeper meaning of the McCarthy episode. He had never met a "red" professor, he said in a speech, but was appalled when he met some revolutionary students during the 'sixties who made it clear that they really did wish to destroy American society and were prepared to use any means available to do it. He had no patience with Sidney Hook, who could have explained to him why an admittedly Communist professor had no right to claim the privilege of academic freedom. He could be arrogant and did not like to be disagreed with. We can admit all that, but also admire him for his untiring, eloquent stand for excellence in education and for the two great speeches at the end of the war, coming as they did after Hiroshima and Nagasaki and in the face of the arrogance of unconditional surrender, when whole nations were being made into penal camps. Those two great speeches could make us feel that there was still hope, that American idealism was more than a propaganda device for ambitious politicians. They were rays of sunlight in a dark and gloomy world, and may well have been the high point of Hutchins' career.

Robert Hutchins was a private person, as one might expect from his family and religious background, but some account of his personal life to add to what has been said of his life as a public person might be in order. It is reported that when it was suggested that he write his memoirs, he replied, "But what could I say about my marriage?" His first marriage to Maude Phelps McVeigh, whom he met during his junior year at Yale at the Long Island house of his father's brother, Frank, a successful New York banker, ended in divorce after twenty-seven years of marriage. There were three daughters with whom Hutchins had a close, affectionate relationship. His wife Maude, from all accounts, was a gifted, ambitious woman, an "artist to her fingertips," as she was described by a close associate of Hutchins. She did good work as a sculptress and was the author of several books, one of which, *A Diary of Love* (1950), attracted a certain amount of attention. She apparently resented being overshadowed by her husband and did not care for the social life demanded of a university president. The temperaments of two strong-willed and gifted personalities, moreover, inevitably led to difficulties. Coming from a close family where the roles of husband and wife were well defined and accepted as a matter of course, Hutchins undoubtedly suffered intensely from the antagonistic situation that developed. After protracted divorce proceedings, in 1949 he married his former secretary, Vesta Orlick, the ceremony performed by his father with his three daughters in attendance.

It was one of Hutchins' qualities of leadership to win the loyalty of those around him, but his only intimate friend was Thornton Wilder. Both were "children of the parsonage," as Hutchins liked to say, and had been friends in school and college. In the memorial address for his old friend, Hutchins said, "For sixty years he was my teacher. His pedagogical methods were irresistible. They were deep personal concern and laughter. . . . He was the best of teachers and the kindest of friends." The years that Wilder taught at the University, 1930 to 1936, as a result of Hutchins' initiative, must have been a rewarding time for both. Wilder was always welcome at the president's house by his wife Maude, who recognized in him a fellow artist. As Hutchins was later to write to his friend, "Those days would have been intolerable without you." The numerous letters to Wilder show Hutchins' need for friendship and support, and give the impression that, for all the respect he enjoyed in the university community, he was a lonely man.

For all the turmoil and violent changes occurring during Hutchins' administration of the University of Chicago—the Great Depression, the Second World War and its aftermath—he never lost his faith in the goal of higher education which, as he never tired of pointing out, is "the training of the mind." There was an unmistakable aura of nobility about Robert Maynard Hutchins that is a reflection of the faith he never surrendered in the higher purpose of education.

Harriet Monroe

Harriet Monroe
and Poetry

CHICAGO'S LITERARY SCENE, such as it was, had brought forth two magazines, *The Chap-Book* and *The Dial*, which, as we have seen, both flourished for a time and then faded away. Harriet Monroe's *Poetry: A Magazine of Verse* has had quite a different and most remarkable history. From its first appearance in late September 1912, and continuing to the present day, this "little magazine" has published and paid for the work of young poets, among them Ezra Pound, T. S. Eliot, Vachel Lindsay, Edgar Lee Masters and Carl Sandburg, in many instances introducing them to the reading public for the first time.

The founder of this unique enterprise, Harriet Monroe, was born in Chicago on December 23, 1860. Her father, Henry Stanton Monroe, was a New Yorker educated as a lawyer. He came to Chicago in 1852, armed with a letter of introduction to Senator Stephen A. Douglas, with whom he developed a close friendship that lasted until Douglas' death in 1861. Her mother's family had come to Chicago in the 1850s, giving them the status of "old settlers," which was helpful no doubt to the daughter in her later career. The family home on South Michigan Avenue was spared in the Great Fire of 1871, but Henry Monroe lost his office, his records and his law library, said to be the best in the West. Even the local insurance company that had covered them was gone. The father never recovered from these losses, going steadily downhill, forfeiting his home and other properties, ending up ill, worn out, living with two of his daughters in a boarding house, a broken man.

His daughter, however, benefited greatly from her father's personal library, reading Shakespeare, the Romantic poets, and the histories of Greece, Rome, and the French Revolution. A quiet, withdrawn girl, she was attracted to the "spectacular heroes" of literature and history, "friends of the spirit," as she describes them, "to easy my loneliness." After a spell of illness and depression, she was sent away at seventeen to be educated at the Visitation Convent, a boarding school in Georgetown. The curriculum was appropriate to a finishing school for young ladies, including composition, languages, music and painting. But she was inspired most by her English teacher, a Sister Paulina. As Harriet Monroe wrote afterwards in her autobiography, *A Poet's Life*, "... a spark from her fire touched off my vague ambitions and warmed up my somewhat frozen youth."

She was later to come across Robert Louis Stevenson's *Prince Otto* and began the process of shifting her interest from historical figures to contemporary heroes, beginning a collection of what she described as her "gallery of personalities." She wrote to Stevenson and received a reply that led to a continuing correspondence. When she finally met the great author, a small, frail shell of a man, she was shocked by the ravages of the disease, tuberculosis, that eventually killed him.

When Harriet Monroe finished school and returned to Chicago, she was forced by her father's reduced circumstances to take a job. She began a career in journalism and in 1888 began her long association with the *Chicago Tribune* as drama and art critic. Oddly, for a young woman of privileged, even sheltered upbringing, she was well prepared for her assignments. Her father had taken her, even at an early age, to the theater where she had seen the great tragedian, Edwin Booth, as Hamlet, admired the famous actress Eleanora Duse and the dancers Nijinsky, Pavlova and Isadora Duncan. Her social position was such that she met the great men of the times as they came to Chicago, Generals Grant and Sherman, William Jennings Bryant, Theodore Roosevelt. Remarkably, for a shy and quiet young woman, it was said of her that "she knew all the leading men and women of Chicago, and was always at the most exclusive functions."

Meanwhile her efforts at poetry were beginning to attract notice. Her first, a sonnet, *With Shelley's Poems*, appeared in the *Century Magazine* in 1889. Three years later her *Valeria and Other Poems* was published and in that same year, 1892, she was commissioned to write a dedicatory cantata for the opening of Adler and Sullivan's Auditorium Building.

The considerable creative ferment, as the city prepared to stage a great fair, the World's Columbian Exposition, gave rise to a variety of cultural activities. But when Harriet Monroe learned that the opening ceremonies, planned as a spectacular event, would celebrate all the arts, music, painting and dance, even architecture, but would ignore poetry, she made up her mind that if no one else was going to do anything about that deplorable omission, then she would. A woman of very definite ideas, Harriet Monroe felt the dedication ceremonies would be incomplete without a commemorative poem and with no other contender in view, she prepared to compose one.

The Committee on Ceremonies for the fair, consisting of eight local members, including Chicago's transit magnate, Charles T. Yerkes, and eight members from other parts of the country, eventually gave way to Harriet Monroe's determination and duly recommended that a poem be read to mark the grand opening and that she be asked to write it. "We shall want a poem that will live," Mr. Yerkes instructed her. *The Columbian Ode*, it was also decided, should include two or three songs for the great chorus of five thousand voices to be conducted by Theodore Thomas. The Chicago exposition was supposed to bring all the nations of the world together and to inaugurate a new era of universal peace and happiness. Thus the concluding verse of the ode includes the following hopeful lines:

Men shall be free forevermore,
And love shall be law supreme.

The dedication ceremonies took place in October 1892, six months before the formal opening of the world exposition. The event was staged in the great hall of the Manufactures and Liberal Arts building, a structure covering some forty-four acres, before an audience of 125,000. In addition to the songs presented by that giant chorus, the other sections of the ode were read by Sarah Cowell LeMoyne, a six-foot-tall actress from New York. The presentation of the ode was received with thunderous applause and two laurel wreaths were bestowed on the reciter of the work and its author. Harriet Monroe also received a fee of $1,000 for her effort, but the pamphlet edition of the ode, which she paid to have printed, did not sell. Still in 1894 she was awarded $5,000 in punitive damages in a suit she brought against the *New York World* for printing the ode without her permission, which perhaps explains how she managed the wherewithall to spend a year and a half in Europe. Throughout her life, in addition to her passion in the cause of poetry, Harriet Monroe was devoted to travel, to seeing the world, and she had a talent for getting other people to pay for her "adventures," as she called them.

As evidence of this rather singular talent, following her European excursion, Harriet Monroe, no doubt depressed by her father's illness and indigence, was taken ill herself. To help her recover, a friend got her a round trip pass on the Santa Fe railroad to Phoenix, Arizona. As she was to write later, "An illness gave me the West—a gift of incalculable value." Her adventure in the Southwest included a stagecoach ride to the Grand Canyon that led to an article, "The Grand Canyon of the Colorado," that appeared in *Atlantic* magazine. And that in turn led to the railroad people offering her passes whenever she wished to venture west again, as she was to do many times, not only to Arizona but to California.

Her everyday life, however, was not satisfying to her. She continued to write on art and drama for the *Tribune* and she taught several afternoons a week at a girls' school. She also wrote a rather long prose poem, *The Hotel*, which was accepted for the *Atlantic Monthly* by the editor Bliss Perry with "particular pleasure," appearing in March 1909. She wrote a children's operetta, "The Troll's Holiday," which was performed with great success at Hull House. Her literary and travel articles appeared in the *Atlantic*, the *Century*, and even London's *Fortnightly Review*. She took part as well in the meetings of The Little Room, which included such members as Henry B. Fuller, a lifelong friend; Roswell Field, Hobart C. Chatfield-Taylor, John and George McCutcheon, Edith Wyatt and Lorado Taft, which made her a member of the most creative group the city had to offer. But pleasant and pleasing as all these activities were, she came to feel that they did not provide the challenge she needed in her years of maturity. Somehow she had the feeling that hers were "empty years." In 1906 she wrote plaintively, "Would I ever do the perfect thing we were all striving for?" As she complains in her autobiography, "Nobody seemed to want very much what I could do; there was no certainty or permanence in any employment, and always, for anything I offered or any job I secured, there was very meager pay." After the triumph of her *Columbian Ode*, she wanted more than anything else to do something important for the art of poetry.

In 1910 Harriet Monroe, armed with assignments from the *Tribune*, determined to travel around the world, a trip that was to include a visit with her sister Lucy, wife of the American minister to Peking, William J. Calhoun. En route she met in London the publisher Elkin Matthews, who thought highly of the work of a young American expatriate living in London, Ezra Pound, whose work he had published. Harriet Monroe records the encounter in her autobiography: " 'That is real poetry!' he exclaimed, as he showed me the *Personae* and *Exaltations*; so I bought the tiny volumes, and later beguiled the long Siberian journey with the strange and beautiful rhythms of this new poet, my self-exiled compatriot."

The visit to Peking was, of course, before the Chinese revolution and, as the guest of the American minister, she could experience the great city as it was in the days of the Chinese empire. Her impressions are contained in the chapter, "The Beauty of Peking," from her autobiography, which reads in part:

> For a fine serenity, a kind of haughty modesty, is the keynote of
> the Chinese ideal of life and art. Their temples are low, not lofty
> like Gothic cathedrals. Their palaces and mandarin homes contain,
> not vast halls, but a maze of smaller rooms around open courts
> which frame the sky. Even their pagodas do not rise very high, and
> the most impressive part of the Temple of Heaven, indeed the very
> flower of Chinese architecture and one of the masterpieces of the
> world, is the circular marble Altar open to the sun and stars,
> which, mounted on its three marble terraces, rises less than twenty
> feet above the triply walled-in level of the park. . . . The feeling is
> one of infinite repose, of a peace beyond thought, beyond desire.
> Here might Nirvana begin for our agitated restless care-laden
> world, here within these triple balustrades and triple walls of this

Temple of Heaven, this complete and consummate artistic expression of the Oriental ideal.

Harriet Monroe returned to Chicago from her stimulating world travel in January 1911. Not surprisingly, she found that continuing her work teaching school and writing critical reviews for the *Tribune* was even less satisfying than before. However, this was apparently a very active period in the city's cultural life. Chicago at the time, she notes in her autobiography, was "surging with art activities and aspirations beneath its commercial surface." Daniel Burnham was pushing ahead with his "Plan of Chicago," the Art Institute under the leadership of Charles L. Hutchinson was adding to its collections and its school was offering scholarships and prizes to young artists. The musical life of the city, under the direction of Frederick Stock, who led the orchestra, and supported by several outstanding conservatories, was also thriving. But despite all the creative energy being expended, Harriet Monroe was quick to realize that nothing was being done for poetry. She notes this niggardly treatment of poets in her autobiography and asks, "Why this difference between the respectful attitude of donors and press and public toward painting and sculpture, also to a certain degree, music and architecture, and the general contemptuous indifference of all these powers toward the poet and the beautiful art he practices or aims at, the art which, more than any other, has passed on the 'tale of the tribe' to succeeding generations? . . . The minor painter or sculptor or architect was receiving every encouragement, from his art-school days onward, to develop his art and become distinguished in it, while the poet, whether minor or major, . . . received no prizes, few magazines would accept his work for anything but page-end 'fillers,' and the checks which rewarded rare acceptances were absurdly and ruinously small.

"Why," she writes indignantly, "was there nothing done for poets, the most unappreciated and ill-paid artists in the world?" She decided during the half-year following her return from her world travel, that something had to be done, and who else was there? Her autobiography notes that "something must be done; and since nobody else was doing anything, it might be 'up to me' to try to stir up the sluggish situation." She concludes, significantly, "Poets needed a magazine, an organ of their own, and I would start one for them." This was, as she indicates elsewhere in her autobiography, "the birth of an idea" and credits the inspiration to her ruminations on that eleven-day train ride, reading Pound and thinking about poetry, from Moscow across Siberia to the Forbidden City of Old Peking.

After discussing the matter with two sympathetic friends, Harriet Monroe made up her mind to take it up with Chatfield-Taylor, her friend from The Little Room. He was a successful and much-respected businessman, socially prominent, and a published novelist. On June 23, 1911, she called upon him and he agreed that the plight of poetry was indeed desperate and that something should be done. She proposed a small monthly magazine be launched that would include a presentation of new poems, editorials and reviews. She felt strongly that all poems should be paid for upon acceptance and that prizes should also be offered from time to time. After considering her proposal, Chatfield-Taylor suggested it ought to be possible to get one hundred subscribers to guarantee $50 a year for five years which would be sufficient to cover printing costs and office expenses. He agreed to begin the subscription list himself and suggested that she go to the architect, Howard Shaw, for the second enrollment. The first pledges came quickly, of course, from people she knew or were impressed by some of the early subscribers, which included Burnham, Glessner, McCormick, Palmer and Pullman. By Christmas she had secured thirty or more subscriptions.

Finally obtaining the one hundred pledges that promised to support her magazine for the first five years, Harriet Monroe then spent two months reading what was available in books and magazines of the work of contemporary poets. From this survey she made a list of the people she would solicit for material to consider for publication, a list that included such names as Floyd Dell, Herman Hagadorn, Vachel Lindsay, Amy Lowell, Percy McKaye, Edwin Markham, Grace Fallow Norton, Ezra Pound, Edwin Arlington Robinson, Louis Untermeyer, George Sylvester Viereck, Edith Wharton, and Helen Hay Whitney. To each she sent her carefully prepared prospectus and was pleased that answers were received from nearly all. Edith Wharton was one of the few who did not reply.

A long and stimulating letter was received from Ezra Pound who in those days, of course, was not as well known as he was to become. He had been teaching at Wabash College in Indiana when he was dismissed for giving shelter overnight to a stranded actress. He took the pay coming to him and went off to Venice, published his first book, *A Leume Sperto*, and settled in England in self-imposed exile, becoming almost immediately a literary celebrity in London. In her letter, Harriet Monroe told him that she had read his poetry on her trip around the world, adding how much she admired his work, which may well have helped to bring on the nearly two-page letter she received in response, the beginning of a long and fruitful association. Pound's first letter begins, "I *am* interested, and your scheme, as far as I understand it, seems not only sound, but the only possible method. There is no other magazine in America which is not an insult to the serious artist and to the dignity of his art."

Pound agreed to act as European correspondent and very soon sent in contributions from Rabindranath Tagore, William Butler Yeats, T. E. Lawrence, and Ford Maddox Hueffer, who was soon to change his name to Ford Maddox Ford. On the subject of Lawrence, Pound writes in a letter dated September 23, 1913: "Lawrence, as you know, gives me no particular pleasure. Nevertheless we are lucky to get him. Hueffer, as you know, thinks highly of him. I *recognize* certain qualities of his work. If I were an editor I should probably accept his work without reading it. As a prose writer I grant him first place among the younger men."

Then, in a letter dated September 30, 1914, Pound writes, "I was jolly well right about Eliot. He has sent in the best poem I have yet had or seen from an American. Pray God it not be a single and unique success. He has taken it back to get it ready for the press and you shall have it in a few days."

Pound was to add, "He is the only American I know of who has made what I can call adequate preparation for writing. He has actually trained himself *and* modernized himself *on his own*. The rest of the promising young have done one or the other but never both (most of the swine have done neither). It is such a comfort to meet a man and not have to tell him to wash his face, wipe his feet, and remember the date (1914) on the calendar."

The letter that follows has no date, saying only, "Here is the Eliot poem. The most interesting contribution I've had from an American. P.S. Hope you'll get it in soon." The submission was *The Love Song of J. Alfred Prufrock*, not printed until June 1915. This would be the first publication in the United States of a poem by Eliot and that it should appear in *Poetry* was, of course, a great coup. But apparently it was to take considerable persuasion on Pound's part to induce Harriet Monroe to accept it. In a letter dated November 9, 1914, Pound writes, "Your letter—the long one—to hand is the most dreary and discouraging document that I have been called upon to read for a very long time.

"Your objection to Eliot is the climax. No—you are not at liberty to say that she is Mrs. F. M. Hueffer. You are especially requested to make no allusion to the connection.

"I think that is all that needs an immediate answer."

But the matter of the publication of *Prufrock* must still not have been settled. Pound was to write again, "No, most emphatically I will not ask Eliot to write down to any audience whatsoever. I dare say my instinct was sound enough when I volunteered to quit the magazine quietly about a year ago. Neither will I send you Eliot's address in order that he may be insulted."

The difference of opinion must have continued as Pound was to write the following observations on January 31, 1915: "Now as to Eliot: 'Mr. Prufrock' does not 'go off at the end.' It is a portrait of failure or of a character which fails, and it would be false art to make it end on a note of triumph. I dislike the paragraph about Hamlet, but it is an early and cherished bit and T. E. won't give it up, and as it is the only portion of the poem that most readers will like at first reading, I don't see that it will do much harm.

"For the rest: a portrait satire on futility can't end by turning that quintessence of futility, Mr. P. into a reformed character breathing fire and ozone."

This seems to have calmed Harriet Monroe's concern about *Prufrock*. Peace was restored, Pound did not "quit the magazine," and the poem, as noted, appeared in *Poetry* in June. It not only was a pioneering effort in modern poetry but it clearly made the magazine's reputation.

In a letter mailed in August, Pound tells her, "I send also the three gems of Eliot for September, and a forthcoming 'Cousin Nancy,' which may do to fill the second page." Only three of the four were printed, *The Boston Evening Transcript, Aunt Helen,* and *Cousin Nancy,* all in *Poetry,* October 1915. This is the *Cousin Nancy,* by the way, that so disturbed Waldo Browne.

Pound not only acted as the unpaid European representative of the magazine, but also, born teacher that he was, didn't hesitate to instruct Harriet Monroe in the art of poetry, as the following from a letter dated January 1915 illustrates:

> Poetry must be *as well written as prose.* Its language must be a fine language, departing in no way from speech save by a heightened intensity (i.e. simplicity). There must be no book words, no paraphrases, no inversions. It must be as simple as DeMaupassant's best prose, and as hard as Stendhal's.

> There must be no interjections. No words flying off to nothing. Granted one can't get perfection every shot, this must be one's intention.

For her part, Harriet Monroe greatly appreciated all that Pound had done for her and the magazine in his poems, his reviews and his letters to her, as the following from her autobiography shows:

> During our first year or two, Ezra's pungent and provocative letters were falling thick as snowflakes.

> Thus began the rather violent, but on the whole salutary, discipline under the lash of which the editor of the new magazine felt herself being rapidly educated, while all incrustations of habit and prejudice were ruthlessly swept away. Ezra Pound was born to be a great teacher. The American universities which, at this time of his developing strength, failed, one and all, to install him as the head of an English department, missed a dynamic influence which would have been felt wherever English writing is taught. It is not entirely his fault if he has become somewhat embittered and has spent

upon trivial quarrels and temperamental exaggerations the energy which should have gone into important progressive work. The power which would have been stimulating has become explosive, and like many another man of genius, Pound has been thwarted and diverted into passionate reactions against human dullness. *Poetry's* first few years came in the period of his greatest power—a controversial statement, perhaps, for those who prefer the *Cantos* to the poems in *Lustra* and earlier volumes. At any rate, *Poetry* was the first of the numerous "little magazines" which he has fostered or founded and then tired of. Its editor has always acknowledged gratefully what she owed to his help during those first diverting and experimental years.

The first issue of *Poetry: A Magazine of Verse* appearing on September 23, 1912, marked Vol. 1, No. 1, October, had an initial press run of 1,000 copies. This was soon sold out and a second printing of 1,000 ordered. The Chicago papers greeted the new magazine in a friendly way, although the *Tribune* noted it was coming out in "the most commercial city of the age." A Philadelphia paper entitled its editorial, "Poetry in Porkopolis." But the *New York Sun* was more cordial in its greeting, as was the *Christian Science Monitor*. Two lines from a poem, *To Whistler—American*, by Pound in the first issue,

> *You and Abe Lincoln from that mass of dolts*
> *Show us there's a chance at least of winning through*

aroused some wrathful correspondence, and the first publication of Carl Sandburg's poem on Chicago as "hog butcher to the world" brought forth the description of "a futile little periodical described as 'a magazine of verse,' " in *The Dial*. But, by this time, it should be remembered, that publication was being edited by the son of the founder.

Still *Poetry* and its creator soon settled into offices in an old remodelled mansion on Cass Street, later North Wabash Avenue, occupying a single front room with a fireplace and a Monroe family heirloom, an antique clock. There were several chairs and desks scattered about, one chair in particular became "the poet's chair," reserved for visiting distinguished guests, but usually occupied by locals, Carl Sandburg, Vachel Lindsay, or Edgar Lee Masters. Later Sherwood Anderson would regularly claim it.

The magazine, meanwhile, was itself to become the home of such diverse talents as Rupert Brooke, Ernest Hemingway, Robinson Jeffers, James Joyce, Joyce Kilmer, Marianna Moore, Wallace Stevens and William Carlos Williams. It achieved perhaps the greatest success of all the so-called "little magazines." But in time its impact and influence seemed to wane. Some twenty years after its founding, at the depths of the Great Depression, Harriet Monroe felt the magazine could not financially survive. It was rescued by a $20,000 grant from the Carnegie Foundation.

The twenty-two years during which Harriet Monroe edited her magazine must have been a wonderfully creative and challenging time in her life. Among the high points were undoubtedly the first publication of T. S. Eliot's work and the dinner held in 1914 in honor of William Butler Yeats, proclaimed "the greatest poet of our time." The affair was held in the Cliff Dwellers Club in Chicago and Yeats who had been given *Poetry's* annual award for his poem, *The Gray Rock*, accepted with the condition that he keep only a small part of the $250 and that the rest be given to Ezra Pound, who, he said, needed it more than he did. Vachel Lindsay was invited also to attend and said he would only if the magazine would pay his fare from Springfield since he had no money. Still he volunteered to read a new poem, not yet published, *The Congo*, which, it should be added, caused a great sensation. The banquet was an impressive occasion, attended by more than a hundred guests, including most of the guarantors of the magazine. Yeats made an eloquent talk, which included the advice:

> Real enjoyment of a beautiful thing is not achieved when a poet
> tries to teach. It is not the business of a poet to instruct his age. He
> should be too humble to instruct his age. His business is merely to
> express himself, whatever that self may be. I would have all Ameri-
> can poets keep in mind François Villon.

At the conclusion of his talk, Yeats read a few poems, which included two by Ezra Pound, *The Ballad of the Goodly Fere* and *The Return*. Of the latter, he remarked, "This last is, I think, the most beautiful poem that has been written in the free form, one of the few in which I find real organic rhythm."

By the time she came to write her autobiography, Harriet Monroe was to regard the dinner for Yeats as "one of my great days, those days which come to most of us as atonement for long periods of drab disappointment or dark despair."

Even in her busy years editing the magazine, Harriet Monroe was able to find the time and the means to travel. The first ten years or so she could manage, with her passes on the railroad, only brief trips to explore the West. In the summer of 1923 she took her first long vacation from *Poetry* with a five-month tour through England, France and Spain, finally meeting Pound in person while in Paris. In 1929 she went to see Egypt's great pyramids and the classic temples of Greece. And in 1933 she went to Mexico to explore the ruins of the ancient Aztec and Mayan civilizations. The next year saw a reunion with her sister in Peking.

Upon her return to Chicago from China, Harriet Monroe began the writing of her autobiography. In 1935, Macmillan published her collected verses, *Chosen Poems*. Then, when she had written her life up to the year 1922, she was appointed a representative to the annual PEN conference to be held that year in Buenos Aires. In August, she took a train to New York and boarded the Grace Lines' *Southern Cross*. In her seventies, she was described by a fellow traveller as "a strange little maiden lady." But she was not as frail as she appeared; Harriet Monroe's strong-featured face still testified to her determination. During the two-week conference, she spoke up only once and then simply to describe her efforts on behalf of poetry through her magazine.

She was not entirely impressed by the proceedings but pleased that it had taken her to a part of the world she had not seen before. Then, rather than return home, Harriet Monroe decided to take the two-day train trip across the Andes to Santiago, Chile. There she joined the *Santa Lucia* which was cruising up the west coast of South America. She disembarked at Mollendo, Peru, and headed for Cuzco, determined to see "the lost city of the Incas," the ruins at Machu Picchu. The journey took her to Arequipa where a rest was scheduled at a local pension in an effort to adjust the travellers to the extremely high altitudes. At 7,500 feet, the altitude proved too much for her, she had a fall, was confined to bed, went into a coma and died, September 26, 1936 of a cerebral hemorrhage.

Her family wished to have her cremated and the ashes returned to Chicago, but upon learning that Peruvian law forbade cremation, decided it was better to have her interred there, her brother declaring it was "better and more in character to have her buried in the highlands of Peru where she died on her last adventure."

Among her papers were found the last pages of her autobiography, a chapter she had entitled "Last Words: Past and Future." They included her comment, "Is it not enough for us that life is magnificent, and now and then it offers golden moments which shake out the soul like a banner in the wind?"

Of all the tributes to her, Ezra Pound's was perhaps the most appropriate: "During the twenty-four years of her editorship ... her magazine provided the most honorable place a poet could be published."

Her grave, in the Arequipa cemetery, beneath the towering peak of El Misti, a magical mountain, bears a simple bronze plaque with the dates of her birth and death and the simple inscription: "Harriet Monroe, POET, Friend of Poets."

PART THREE

A Consideration
of Three Chicago
Authors

Henry Blake Fuller

Henry Blake Fuller:
The Unwilling Chicagoan*

ENRY FULLER, born in Chicago in 1857, was not the first Chicago writer, but the first Chicago writer to win national recognition as a literary figure. At a time when the rugged early days of Chicago were still alive in the memories of those who had experienced them, its history became the subject of a number of books and pamphlets, one of the first Juliette Magill Kinzie's *Narrative of the Massacre at Chicago, August 15, 1812.* It was based on the recollections, among others, of her mother-in-law Eleanor Kinzie, and published as a pamphlet in 1844. This was later included in a book, *Wau-Bun,* which was an account of the author's move to Chicago from the East as the bride of John H. Kinzie and published ten years later in 1856. After the Great Fire of 1871, Robert Fergus, one of the first printers in Chicago, collected as many such first-hand accounts as he could find to preserve the early history of the city and published them as pamphlets in his Fergus Historical Series, as cited earlier. Worthy as all this was, it was little more than local history. It was only the founding in 1880 of its first, and unfortunately last, successful literary magazine, *The Dial,* the establishment of several publishing firms, the arrival of such men as George Ade, Eugene Field and Hamlin Garland, and the recognition accorded to Henry Fuller, who was not only born in Chicago but was a third-generation Chicagoan, that it can be said that Chicago could make some claim to be a literary center.

Henry B. Fuller's grandfather, also Henry Fuller, was born in Northampton, Massachusetts in 1805. He came from a successful and distinguished New England family. He was a direct descendent of Samuel Fuller, who had arrived on the *Mayflower,* and was a first cousin of the writer Margaret Fuller. After founding a tannery in New York State and then becoming a judge in St. Joseph, Michigan,

* From a paper read before The Chicago Literary Club on January 13, 1992.

this early Fuller settled in Chicago in 1849. Soon after arriving, he set himself up in the horse-drawn streetcar business, which involved the usual political negotiations for the necessary franchises, and from there went into railroads, becoming a founder of the Rock Island road and acquiring a substantial fortune in the process. The Fuller family, having experienced the tumultuous rise of Chicago from rough frontier village to thriving metropolis, with the riots, panics, and Great Fire that accompanied the rise, felt themselves a part of that rather select group of "Old Settlers," who were inclined to hold themselves somewhat apart from later arrivals. The house where Fuller was born and grew up stood on Van Buren Street, occupying the site where the LaSalle Street Station was later to be built.

Fuller is described as a shy, introspective man, small of stature, compact, witty, a keen observer of the world around him, and much liked by those able to penetrate his reserve and win his friendship. His close friend Hamlin Garland, in his book of reminiscences, *Roadside Meetings*, said of him: "He wore at this time a full brown beard and carried himself with a fastidious grace, a small, alert gentleman who resented the mental and physical bad smells and the raucous noises of his native town. . . . He said little and his sentences were short, precisely controlled, and pertinent. He had little patience with fuzzy pretentiousness." First sent to a Chicago public school, he then spent a year at a private academy in Oconomowoc, Wisconsin, which was a happy time for him. After this school was discontinued, he went back to a Chicago high school, where he finished at the top of his class. In accordance with his father's wish that he go into business, after finishing school he went to work in a crockery store, which he hated. He spent his leisure hours following a rigid course in reading, which included Dickens, Johnson's *Rasselas*, and Gibbon's *Decline and Fall*. He also translated Goethe and Schiller into blank verse. As he remarked in his diary, he was determined to make himself "A master of the English tongue." His biographer, John Pilkington, Jr., says of him following his graduation from South Division High School, "In addition to his knowledge of Latin literature, Fuller had read widely in the English, German and French classics. He was a trained musician and an advanced student of musical composition. Finally, he could write English with a precision and style characteristic of a professional writer."

After a year doing clerical work in the crockery store, Fuller secured a job at the bank where his father was vice president. Here he spent about eight months, at first as a messenger and then as a clerk. During all this time, he dreamed of travel in order, as his biographer put it, "to learn the secrets of civilization." Italy was his goal, for which he prepared himself with meticulous care, among other ways by the study of architecture. He also studied guide books and maps of the cities he planned to visit. By the time he set off on his first trip to Europe at the age of twenty-two in 1879, Fuller knew exactly where he wanted to go and what he wanted to see. He landed in Liverpool on August 30, 1879, and, after visiting Chester, Coventry, Warwick Castle, Stratford-on-Avon, and Oxford, arrived in London on September 7. In London he visited all the places a conscientious traveller was expected to see: the Houses of Parliament, Westminster Abbey, the Crystal Palace, Kew Gardens, the British Museum, Chancery Lane, Hyde Park, the Guildhall, and, after each exhausting day, he carefully noted down his impressions. He called St. Paul's "Wren's great classic sham," and observed, after his visit to the National Gallery, "I had to give it up—the Old Masters are too many for me." After three weeks in England, he went on to Paris. He felt uncomfortable in the Louvre—he lacked sympathy for French painting and sculpture—but was greatly impressed by Notre Dame: "The front is the finest Gothic composition that I may ever hope to see. . . . the three rose windows are probably unrivaled in the gracefulness of their tracery and the gloriousness of their coloring." But Versailles, on the other hand, he found "dull" and "hateful." The night he left Paris heading for Rome, he asked in his journal, "What, after all, is civilization?" The beginning of an answer, he hoped to find at last in Italy.

While Rome was his ultimate objective, Fuller stopped in Genoa, Pisa, Florence, Siena and Orvieto. Genoa delighted him, but while he was impressed by the architecture of Florence, his New England inheritance and Chicago background had left him unprepared for the "evil of such promiscuous nudity as meets the eye at every turn." Rome, where he arrived on December 6, staying until March 8,

1880 was overwhelming to him. Day after day, whatever the weather, he explored the city and, by the time he left, as he wrote in his notebook, "With the exception of some few odds and ends, I have seen everything of Rome within the walls, and have lately been giving some attention to the sights beyond them." His New England Protestant upbringing made it difficult for him to appreciate St. Peter's: "Aesthetically, St. Peter's is wholly pagan. Morally, St. Peter's is glorification of a dis-christianized Papacy." Even the Sistine Chapel did not escape his censure, but for all that, he remarked in his diary, the magnificence of Rome is "inexhaustible."

The Italian cities of the time of Fuller's visit, not yet overrun by cars and hordes of tourists, were still as Ruskin and Goethe had found them. One can imagine the impression they made on a perceptive, romantically inclined young man newly arrived from Chicago, a city the realistic Hamlin Garland described in those days as ". . . an ugly, smoky, muddy town built largely of wood and without a single beautiful structure. . . . Miles of the streets were lined with smoke-blackened wooden houses, set high as if to avoid spring floods. In rainy times the downtown pavements were deep with a slimy mixture of mud and soot."

After leaving Rome in March 1880, Fuller travelled through the cities of northern Italy. He spent eighteen days in Venice and again visited Florence, this time making a careful examination of the Campanile. "I was pleased," he wrote in his notebook, "to find the workmanship of the Campanile most honest, thorough, and finished. . . . The Campanile was built on thoroughly medieval principles; Giotto did not give the best he could for the money, but his absolute best." The cities of northern Italy appealed to him as much as those he had visited earlier; Assisi he particularly admired, as he said, for its "air of honest reality."

Switzerland, after Italy, was "a blessed relief" but for Fuller, less inspiring than Italy. He was disappointed by Munich, but most impressed by the Passion Play at Oberammergau, which, he thought, demonstrated ". . . the art that lies so close to nature as to hardly be distinguished from it." On August 19, 1880 he sailed for home, having spent almost exactly one year in Europe. When he arrived in his native city a few weeks later it was to see it through very different eyes from when he had left. He was now faced with the same problem as many other young Americans who have had a similar experience: adjusting himself to American life with the experience of European culture behind him.

The first year or two after Fuller's return must have been an especially difficult time for him. His interests had little in common with those of his parents, his European experience had made him more than ever unfitted for business, and he probably knew no one in Chicago he could even talk to about the subject that concerned him: how to lead a civilized life in modern America. In April 1883 he was off again to Europe, following somewhat the same pattern as his earlier trip, but this time staying only until September. Although he had undertaken the trip to flee from what he doubtless considered the "philistinism" of Chicago, it seems to have made him realize that Europe might not after all be the solution he was seeking. In any case, upon his return, perhaps with the hope that William Dean Howells' example might provide him with an answer to his problem, he spent a year in Boston.

Fuller's career as a professional writer began during his time in Boston with the sale of four humorous pieces (one a parody of Bret Harte) to the newly founded *Life* magazine. The illness and death of his father in early 1885 brought him back to Chicago, where he was needed to look after his invalid mother and to take care of his father's estate. By the time the estate was finally settled, little more was left of the fortune his grandfather had accumulated than a number of modest rental properties, the management of which remained a burden for Fuller the rest of his life. It was at this time that he began to consider the careers of Henry James and William Dean Howells, and particularly the manner each had chosen—James as an expatriate, Howells as an American writer—to make his way after having experienced the seductions of Europe. Fuller's conclusion is brought out in an essay written at this time, "Howells or James?" which remained unpublished until 1957. The essay begins with the question, ". . . which of these two representative writers is to be pronounced most instrumental in the shaping of American fiction, and which of them will ultimately come to be recognized as most firmly and completely a factor in an historical American literature?" However reluctantly, and "notwithstanding his very exceptional gifts and his score of delightful qualities," Fuller came to the conclusion that of the two, Howells, or James, it would be the expatriate James who would be less instrumental in the shaping of American fiction.

Having come down on the side of the realistic Howells, Fuller proceeded to write a book, *The Chevalier of Pensieri-Vani*, which, surprisingly, appears to be completely in the manner of Henry James. It is neither a novel nor a travel book, although it has elements of both, rather, the book is an imaginative, evocative account of a leisurely journey through a number of Italian cities by a group of friends, each one more distinctly an individual than the next. It is a unique party, perhaps conceivable only in the mind of a romantic American in pre-industrial Italy. They visit different cities and encounter various situations. The purpose of the author in all this, it would seem, was to demonstrate civilized life as it had evolved over the centuries in the cities of Italy.

The *Chevalier* was written in 1886—1887, a time of tension and depression for Fuller, when the decision whether or not he would spend his life in Chicago seemed to have been decided for him by forces over which he had no control. He began the book, he wrote later, for his own amusement during the lunch hour while working in a Chicago office, extracting old envelopes for the purpose from a wastebasket. In the first paragraph, which sets the tone of the entire book, we meet a Chevalier, who, the author tells us, he ". . . scarce need confess, was a 'poor gentleman'—one with much, perhaps, behind him, but very little by him, and not much more before him. But he loved the post-roads of Tuscany and the soft vowels of the bocca Romana, and every spreading pine-tree and every antique stone of the fair Italian land. He had very little money and little prestige, but he was young, and he was happy, too, in an abundance of leisure and a disposition to follow the byways with content. And he was on his way to Rome."

We soon meet the Chevalier's friend, the Seigneur de Hors-Concours, who possesses a small patrimony in the Alps of Savoy which has been in his family some seven hundred years. They had become friends, several years before, when both were making a careful study of the Cathedral of Orvieto, when the Chevalier on the occasion of a great religious festival was asked by the Bishop to improvise on the organ, the regular organist being indisposed, which he did with such astonishing virtuosity that he was rewarded in Rome with a title. Another member of the company, who plays a major part in their adventures, in the Prorege, the Viceroy of Arcopia, an island in the Adriatic, who, with great dignity and self-assurance, represents the principle of aristocracy. For such destructive innovations as democracy, equality, representative government, he has no patience whatever.

The Prorege, to explain his presence on the mainland, had undertaken an excursion in the valley of the Po to find a model for the municipal building he wished to build in Arcopia and present to his loyal subjects. He had invited a young American, George Occident, to join his party for the purpose of instructing this promising young barbarian, as he considered him to be, in some of the elements of Italian culture, chiefly architecture. The need for such instruction had become strikingly clear to the Prorege when, in answering his invitation to join the party, Occident had replied that he would come, "if he could 'find the time'." It seemed strange to the Prorege, "that a young man possessing a fortune of as many millions of lire as Occident was known to enjoy should have difficulty in 'finding time' for any plan that he might set on foot. To him the only man to be envied was the man whose time was in some degree his own; and the most pitiable object that civilization could offer was the rich man a slave to his chronometer."

The Prorege's disquisition on leisure was followed by an equally eloquent expression of his views on the subject of privacy, which had been prompted by the intimation that Occident had sent "a full synopsis of his own intended movements to the public prints." Occident responded with the information that in the community from which he came, "nothing was more public than privacy, nothing more ostentatious than reticence, nothing more calculated to draw the unfavorable notice of the community than any attempt at seclusion." At this the "perplexed Prorege" began "to feel for the first time the magnitude of the task he had undertaken."

The Prorege felt equally strongly on the subject of industrialism and the devastation of nature which came with it:

Whose was the earth? our indignant prince would ask himself
when considerations of this kind rose up to irritate him. Was it the
exclusive possession of those merely who were now living out
their brief day upon it, or was it something more,—the foothold
and heritage of generations yet to come? Who would make good to
those of the coming century the felled trees, the gashed and leveled
hills, the polluted ponds and choked-up streams that signalized our
present dealings with outraged and suffering Mother Nature? Who
was to render back to them an earth as beautiful as that which we
ourselves received as our right,—an earth whose possession and
enjoyment is as much, as inalienably, their right as ours?

After a trip from the mainland on the Prorege's yacht, the company spent a few days in Arcopia, which provided the opportunity
for a discussion of such subjects as the state, the nature of authority
and the source of order in society, subjects on which the Prorege,
needless to say, had opinions which Occident found difficult to
reconcile with the views he had brought with him from his native
city.

The book ends with the return of the Chevalier to his modest
apartment in Florence, where Occident appears one day to inform
him of his decision to return immediately to Shelby County, having
in the meantime taken a wife. A far more devastating blow was a
visit from his old friend Hors-Concours bringing the news that "he,
too, had serious intentions of a matrimonial nature." The Chevalier
consoles himself for all this with the reflection that:

> He could still congratulate himself on his exemption from the bur-
> dens of wealth, the chafings of domestic relations, the chains of
> affairs, the martyrdom of a great ambition, and the dwarfing pro-
> vincialism that comes from one settled home. Others might falter;
> but he was still sufficient unto himself, still master of his own time
> and his own actions, and enamored only by that delightful land
> whose beauty age cannot wither and whose infinite variety custom
> can never stale.

Having finished the book, Fuller wished to see it in print, but he
had some difficulty finding a publisher, which was not too surpris-

ing, not only because of its rather unusual nature, but also because much of it was still written on the backs of old envelopes. He did finally find a small firm in Boston willing to publish it provided he paid the cost. That it was a Boston firm was fortunate, because a copy, by way of the Old Corner Bookstore, came into the hands of Charles Eliot Norton at Harvard, who was then a major influence in literary matters. He, in turn, gave a copy as a Christmas gift to James Russell Lowell who, as Norton had done, wrote a letter to Fuller expressing his high opinion of his work. A review in the *Boston Transcript* followed on February 12, 1891. The *Boston Gazette* concluded its review with the unkind remark that the book would make the author "famous everywhere except in Chicago. There is nothing in Chicago so unlike Chicago as *The Chevalier of Pensieri-Vani*." Other reviewers found it hard to believe that an author who could write a book of such distinction could come from Chicago, which one reviewer described as "that most Godless, lawless, metropolitan, democratic Nazareth"; the *Boston Transcript*, not surprisingly, detected a New England grandfather. After the first publisher, J. J. Cupples & Company, had gone through three editions, Fuller transferred publication to the Century Company, who brought out a new, revised fourth edition, which is dedicated to "that early and indulgent reader . . . to whose kindness its first success is largely due."

Whatever the astonishment of the eastern reviewers that such a work as *The Chevalier* could have come out of Chicago, the book, while not about Chicago, is in fact a reflection of Chicago, and could only have been written in Chicago. The city is never mentioned except once as "Dearborn," the place of origin of "the promising young barbarian," George W. Occident, but we can be sure that when Fuller speaks about the architecture envisioned by the Prorege as "having the effect of massive dignity and spacious splendour," the drab, uninspiring, contemporary architecture of his native city was before his eyes.

The second of Fuller's "leisurely romances of Europe," *The Chatelaine of La Trinité*, was published by the Century Company in 1892, two years after the original publication of his first book. In its style the second book is similar to its predecessor: elegant, precise, with touches of Fuller's characteristic irony. The names of the characters are reminiscent too of those of the first book: Baron Zeitgeist, Marchese of Tempo Rubato, Duke of Largo, Fin-de-Siecle, Professor Saitoutetplus, Mme. Pasdenom. But outwardly similar as they are, they are quite different in their substance. The *Chatelaine*, in contrast to the *Chevalier*, has a plot, is more structured, and has a more clearly stated theme. It is still, outwardly, a travel book, but rather than the cities of Italy which inspired Fuller's passionate admiration, the locale is the Alps, for which his admiration was more reserved. It is a beautiful book, full of unexpected adventures, delightful incidents and telling observations, but it is drier than the first, one can say, perhaps, less lighthearted.

As evidence of how different the second book is from the first, the Prorege of the *Chevalier*, that wonderfully dignified symbol of the principle of aristocracy, has been replaced as the dominant character by a rich, self-confident young American, Aurelia West, who firmly believes that the young woman is the cornerstone, as Fuller puts it, of the social edifice, and that she, Aurelia, has a mission to hasten the Americanization of Europe, which she believes its impending fate to be. The story revolves around her efforts to teach the Chatelaine, who comes from a distinguished old family and is herself an unassuming, healthy mountain girl, whose given name is Bertha, to conduct herself in a way which Aurelia believes is fitting for a member of the European aristocracy.

Before we reach the climax of the story, the reader is entertained by a number of amusing incidents associated with Aurelia's plans to change the demeanor of the Chatelaine from that of modest mountain girl to one she thinks appropriate of the demanding aristocrat. Aurelia, for example, "who was always rendered restless and uneasy by the vicinity of vendible merchandise," at the first opportunity communicates to the Chatelaine "a touch of the subtle poison of shopping." And, while on a mountain excursion with Zeitgeist and his friends, she suggests that her charge, "most robust and tireless of walkers—should be transported in a *chaise à porteur*—a novel experience for the Chatelaine, but one that having tried she was quite willing to repeat. . . . The Chatelaine fell into this new pose quite easily; it did not seem very difficult for her to lean back among her cushions and nod and beckon and command."

During the course of their travels in the Alps, Aurelia is made to suffer in silence a number of pointed remarks about the tyranny of the American aristocracy. Finally she declares that there is no aristocracy in America: the aristocracy of slavery was dead and gone; the aristocracy of intellect had never existed, there or anywhere else, for that matter; and as for the wealthy, it was a simple matter of here today and gone tomorrow, and might well be trusted to dispose of itself. To all this Zeitgeist readily agrees, but then goes on to point out:

> . . . why should anybody be deceived into imagining that a vast, settled, complicated society—a society largely urban and daily becoming more so—could not but develop privilege, draw lines, and bring on the elevation of the *aristos* in one shape or another? The ultimate reaching of such a state was, under ordinary human conditions, unavoidable, and America, as far as his observation went, was now suffering under the rule of an aristocracy novel, indeed, but incredibly widespread, close-knit, firm-rooted, all-pervasive, and ultra-tyrannical—the aristocracy of sex.

While delivering himself of these observations, Zeitgeist, after polishing his spectacles and giving Aurelia "a sharp and sudden look," went on:

> What was American society, Mademoiselle, but a magnificent galley in which husbands and fathers toiled at the oars, while wives and daughters sat above in perfumed idleness? . . . And yet it was in such a land as that—the veritable paradise of women—that the abhorrent reptile of female suffrage had reared its hideous head and had dared to hiss out its demand for "equal rights."

What was expected to be her final triumph, when Aurelia presented the transformed Chatelaine to the three young men who had known and admired her before, turns out to be a disaster. "Where, asked Fin-de-Siecle, was that naïveté, so grateful to the jaded man of the world (he meant himself), the only thing capable of soothing his wearied spirit? What, asked Zeitgeist, had become of the sturdy helpfulness which had no need to make a man into a lackey, and which no person of sense and capability could undervalue? Whither, asked Tempo-Rubato, had vanished that simple innocence which even the greatest reprobate among men admired and respected beyond the vastest store of knowledge that woman could amass?"

As the above makes clear, *The Chatelaine of La Trinite*, like its predecessor, *The Chevalier of Pensieri-Vani*, was not so much concerned with Europe, as with America.

Having established himself as a respected writer with his two romances on the cities of Italy and the Alps, Fuller followed with a realistic novel of Chicago, *The Cliff-Dwellers*. This was published in 1893, no doubt intentionally in the year of Chicago's great triumph, the World's Columbian Exposition, when for one summer Chicago occupied center stage.

The starting point of the novel and the center that brings the characters together is a large, modern office building to which Fuller gives the name of the Clifton. For Fuller such a building was doubtless as representative of the spirit of the modern commercial city, and especially Chicago, as were the cathedrals of Orvieto and Siena of the culture of the Italian cities he so much admired. "The tribe inhabiting the Clifton," as Fuller described them, "is large and rather heterogeneous. All told, it numbers about four thousand souls. It includes bankers, capitalists, lawyers, 'promoters'; brokers in bonds, stocks, pork, oil, mortgages; real-estate people. . . ." They would all fit the description that a character in Fuller's next Chicago novel applies to his fellow citizens in general: "It is the only great city in the world to which all its citizens have come for the one common, avowed object of making money."

The dominant personality in the book, Erastus M. Brainard, came originally from the southernmost part of Illinois, "Egypt," and is owner of the bank located in the Clifton. "He had never lived for anything but business. He had never eaten and drunk for anything but business—his family shared his farm-like fare and his primitive hours. He had never built for anything but business; though constantly investing in grounds and buildings, he had occupied his own home for fifteen years as a tenant merely, before he could bring himself to a grudging purchase." There is George Ogden, who has recently come to Chicago from New England and has begun to work in the Brainard bank. He makes an unfortunate marriage to an empty-headed girl, whose extravagant social ambitions bring about their ruin and provide the climax of the book, and there is the owner of the building whose wife is the society leader of the city and the inspiration of Ogden's wife. Characteristic of Chicago of that day is the real estate man—"His nose was sharp; his eyes were like two gimlets. The effect of his presence was nervous, excitant, dry to acidity." Of all the characters in the book there is only one, Abby, the oldest daughter of Brainard, whom Ogden finally marries after the death of his first wife, who has sufficient character to arouse the sympathy of the reader, but the book ends with their marriage, so we are given no idea of what sort of person she might have become. How successful Fuller was in picturing Chicago is shown by this description of the west side:

> The thousands of acres of ramshackle that made up the bulk of the city, and the tens of thousands of raw and ugly and half-built prairie that composed its environs, seemed together to constitute a great checker-board over whose squares of 'section' and 'township' keenness and rapacity played their daring and wary game. And through the middle of the board ran a line, a hinge, a crack—the same line that loomed up in all those various deeds and abstracts of his with the portentousness and unescapability of the equator—the 'line of the third principal meridian.'

In the reply of the architect of the Clifton to the visitor who expressed admiration for the elevators, Fuller is equally unequivocal about the state of the arts in Chicago:

> "That's all a building is nowadays—one mass of pipes, pulleys, wires, tubes, shafts, chutes, and what not, running through an iron cage of from fourteen to twenty stages. Then the artist comes along and is asked to apply the architecture by festooning on a lot of tile, brick, and terra-cotta. And over the whole thing hovers incessantly the demon of Nine-per-cent."

After this outburst the architect goes on to say:

> "I've got fifteen draughtsmen up under the roof of the Clifton.
> When a new one comes, I say, 'My dear boy, go in for mining or
> dredging, or build bridges, or put up railroad sheds, if you must;
> but don't go on believing that architecture nowadays has any great
> place for the artist.' "

Fuller's second Chicago novel, *With the Procession*, published in
1895, presents as realistic a picture of Chicago as *The Cliff-
Dwellers*, if quite different in spirit. It is a tribute to Fuller's skill as a
writer that two books devoted to the same subject could be so
different in style, but in each case a style perfectly suited to its
subject. The characters who make up *The Cliff-Dwellers*, are all, as
mentioned before, from somewhere else. They are mostly aggressive
types, attracted to Chicago by its spectacular growth and the promise of affluence, without roots in the city. The second book, by way
of contrast, is a story of "old settlers," who are inclined to think of
their city as they knew it in their youth, "before the fire," a city of
congenial neighborhoods, where life seemed predictable, rather
than the great noisy booming city that had taken its place, full of
strange types from who knows where. Fuller's close friend, Hamlin
Garland, had this to say about *With the Procession* in his book of
reminiscences, *Roadside Meetings*, published thirty-five years later:

> Social Chicago of the nineties lies in these pages, more perfectly
> preserved than in any other story then or since. It is a transcript of
> life as Fuller saw it and lived it. It has humor, understanding, and a
> nipping irony. The author not only knew his material; he had
> shared it. Born in Chicago when it was a small town, just before
> the Civil War, he had grown up with it, and in this story he had
> put much that was family history and something that was inti-
> mately autobiographic. . . .

The book revolves around David Marshall, a successful wholesale grocery merchant, and his family. The neighborhood of their
large comfortable home, built during the early years of the Civil
War, has become completely commercialized, their church with
their neighbors had moved three miles south years before, and the

currant bushes that supplied the fruit for Eliza Marshall's annual ritual of jelly making have finally succumbed to the soot and smoke of the city, but it never occurs to them to move, although they have ample means to do so. "Eliza Marshall's Chicago was the Chicago of 1860, an Arcadia which, in some dim and inexplicable way had remained for her an Arcadia still—bigger, noisier, richer, yet different only in degree, and not essentially in kind. She herself had traversed these same streets in the days when they were the streets of a mere town . . . though the *urbs in horto* of the earlier time existed only in the memory of 'old settlers' and in the devise of the municipal seal, while the great Black City stood out as a threatening and evil actuality."

The novel begins with a characteristic Chicago scene of that day, the horse-drawn traffic crossing a bridge over the Chicago River:

The grimy lattice-work of the drawbridge swung to slowly, the steam-tug blackened the dull air and roiled the turbid water as it dragged its schooner on towards the lumber-yards of the South Branch, and a long line of waiting vehicles took up their interrupted course through the smoke and the stench as they filed across the stream into the thick of business beyond: first a yellow street-car; then a robust truck laden with rattling sheet-iron, or piled high with fresh wooden pails and willow baskets; then a junk-cart bearing a pair of dwarfed and bearded Poles, who bumped in unison with the jars of its clattering springs; then, perhaps, a bespattered buggy, with reins jerked by a pair of sinewy and impatient hands. Then more street-cars; then a butcher's cart loaded with carcasses of calves—red, black, piebald—or an express wagon with a yellow cur yelping from its rear; then, it may be, an insolently venturesome landau, with crested panel and top-booted coachman. Then drays and omnibuses and more street-cars; then, presently, somewhere in the line, between the tail end of one truck and the menacing tongue of another, a family carry-all— a carry-all loaded with its family, driven by a man of all work, drawn by a slight and amiable old mare, and encumbered with luggage which shows the labels of half the hotels of Europe.

This is the family of David Marshall, bringing their second son Truesdale home from the station after a four-year stay in Europe.

David Marshall is a conscientious, honest man—a responsible citizen. He goes to bed at nine-thirty so that he can be at his place of business the next morning at seven-thirty, ready to take care of the people who look to him for their supplies of tea, coffee, flour, baking powder, and sugar. Fuller must have known many such men among the acquaintances of his father and grandfather—it was such men who made Chicago. David Marshall managed his life as he did because, as Fuller says, "it was the only thing he could do; because it was the only thing he was pleased and proud to do; because it was the sole thing which enabled him to look upon himself as a useful, stable, honored member of society." He was not endowed with a lively imagination nor an urge to change the world, but with his family, his poor relations, his employees and their families and poor relations, some five or six hundred people were dependent on him for their livelihood. When his son Truesdale after two years at Yale wished to go off to Europe for study, he gave him the necessary letter-of-credit, with what misgivings may be judged by his reply to a friend who had asked about his other son, a lawyer: "He has never had any of the disadvantages of European travel."

When Truesdale stepped from the family carry-all to the carriage block after arriving home from his four years in Europe, he murmured, "Just the same old place. Wonderful how we contrive to stand stock-still in the midst of all this stir and change!" to which his sister Jane added, "just wait and see!" It is Truesdale and Jane, as might be expected, who supply most of the momentum for the story. Truesdale makes it plain to his father that he has no intention of going into the family business, but soon finds himself asking the question, "For what can a man of leisure do, after all, in such a town as this?" He soon discovers that there are no cafes to provide pleasant opportunities for conversation, no artist studios in which to meet interesting and stimulating people, he quickly runs through the available restaurants. While the young men he meets are friendly, they are busy in the occupations of a commercial city— none of them is a man of leisure. "I declare . . . take it altogether, and it's enough to drive a man—to business."

Jane Marshall, who is about thirty-five and still unmarried, has recently called on Mrs. Granger Bates to raise money for a center for working girls, an event which not only changes the course of her life, but that of the rest of the family as well. Mrs. Bates is the acknowledged social leader of Chicago, and having been a friend of Jane's father when both were young and Chicago was the "Arcadia" the old settlers like to remember, receives her cordially. Mrs. Bates is a strong character, proud that her father was a "boss carpenter" and she a schoolteacher, proud of the success of her husband and of their position as leading citizens. She shows Jane through her large and elaborate house—the ballroom, the music room, the formal dining room, the "Louis quinze" drawing room— and when showing her their art collection remarks, "We haven't got any Millet yet, but that morning thing over there is a Corot—at least, we think so . . . after all, people of our position would naturally be expected to have a Corot." She finally takes Jane to her own "small, cramped, low-ceiled room which was filled with worn and antiquated furniture." This was her own room, a replica of the room she had as a girl in her father's house. It was here she could be herself rather than feel that she was the slave of her social secretary and of her servants. Here she could play *Old Dan Tucker* and *The Java March* on her old upright piano, which she would never have felt comfortable doing in their formal music room; here she could read the books she liked rather than the leather-bound classics in uniform editions locked in glass cases in the library. For all that, the expensive formality of their elegant house was important to her because it secured her position as the social leader of Chicago. However straightforwardly honest and unpretentious in her midwestern way she may have been, it was her motto, as she told Jane, to "keep up with the procession . . . and head it if you can," to which she added, "I *do* head it, and I feel that I'm where I belong."

Mrs. Bates takes Jane in hand, shows her how to dress and arrange her hair to better advantage, arranges for her and her brother to attend the great annual ball in the new Auditorium Theater and for her much prettier younger sister to be properly presented to society. David Marshall soon finds himself paying for a fashionable landau to replace the family carry-all and a fine horse to replace the patient Mabel, all of which he accepts without complaint, but also with some question about what it is all for and where it might end. Finally, under the constant pressure of Jane and the inescapable fact that the old neighborhood has become uninhabitable, they employ a fashionable architect to build a new house farther south on Michigan Avenue. The book ends with the death of David Marshall in his unfinished new house where he feels himself a total stranger, the betrothal of Jane to a long-time suitor, and Truesdale's decision to go to Japan to escape Chicago and some sort of complication, never fully explained, but involving, not surprisingly, a young woman of foreign extraction.

Henry Fuller knew the people and the city he writes about, and doubtless has given us an authentic picture of upper middle-class Chicago society as it was in the 1890s and in many ways still is, except that the descendants of Mrs. Bates had moved to Lake Forest. The Marshall family in their comfortable old house in a neighborhood that had seen better days is no doubt in some degree modelled after Fuller's own family, and the frustrations experienced by Truesdale after his exposure to European culture must reflect Fuller's own frustrations, although it should be remembered that Truesdale was a complete, unabashed dilettante, which Fuller was not. In the reflections, however, which he ascribes to Truesdale after visiting what was left of the recently closed World's Fair we can plausibly assume that Fuller is speaking for himself:

> The great town . . . sprawled and coiled about him like a hideous monster—a piteous, floundering monster, too. It almost called for tears. Nowhere a more tireless activity, nowhere a more profuse expenditure, nowhere a more determined striving after the ornate, nowhere a more undaunted endeavor towards the monumental expression of success, yet nowhere a result so pitifully grotesque, grewsome, appalling.

The publication of these two realistic novels describing life in Chicago brought forth very different responses from the two leisurely romances of Europe. "Most of his fellow citizens," according to Bernard K. Bowron, "did not recognize *The Cliff-Dwellers* to be anything but an unqualified blast at the city's reputation." Mary

Abbott, the critic of the *Chicago Post* who had enthusiastically praised his first book and eloquently defended Chicago against the slurs contained in the review of it in the *Boston Gazette*, was of the opinion that Fuller in his new book was "treacherously deficient in sympathy," and that his attack on business was "a piece of mere personal alienation." *The Dial*, on the other hand, which had a national rather than a local circulation, greeted this evidence of Fuller's conversion from romanticism to realism with approval: "An alert and unsentimental depiction of everyday life in the newest great city of the New World. . . . Mr. Fuller appears to be one of the few people who can judge with objective fairness of the community in which their lives have been spent. His book seems to us to have no less value as a document than as a story." William Dean Howells' favorable review in *Harper's Weekly*, a copy of which he sent to Fuller with a friendly letter, included the remark, "As yet no New Yorker has done so much for New York; no Bostonian for Boston."

With the Procession, in contrast to *The Cliff-Dwellers*, was greeted warmly in Chicago. The review in *The Dial*, which had also liked *The Cliff-Dwellers*, began, "We are almost inclined to think that Chicago had found what Carlisle would have called a Voice." *The Chap-Book*, Chicago's other literary magazine in those dim and distant days when Chicago had two, began an appreciative review with the words, "He has been kinder to us in this venture than he was in *The Cliff-Dwellers*. . . . What a debt we owe to the native pride of Mr. Fuller, which so assuredly stamps him as one of us. . . . The book is written with a master hand. Mr. Fuller's grasp upon our municipal life is amazing in its strength and virility." James Huneker was of the opinion that while "less forceful than *The Cliff-Dwellers*," *With the Procession* was "finer in its art, its characterization and development."

The review of the book in *Harpers Weekly*, by William Dean Howells, included the observation: "I do not know how conscious Mr. Fuller may have been in his fealty to Chicago when he was writing his story, but it seems to me that I have never read a book more intensely localized, that is to say, realized . . . perhaps it is well that for the present at least his sense of Chicago should be so critical. . . . Criticism is merely the expression of thorough understanding." He concludes, "At present we have no one to compare with him in the East, in scale and quality of work." Howells particularly liked Mrs. Granger Bates, whom he included in his book, *Heroines of Fiction*.

One of the most perceptive observations about Fuller's new book came from Charles Eliot Norton, who, it will be remembered, discovered Fuller's first book and brought him to the attention of the Boston and New York reviewers. After raising the question whether describing the lives of rather ordinary people, as Fuller does in his two Chicago novels, is the best work an artist can do for his city, Norton goes on to observe, "I believe that your 'Chevalier' has done more for Chicago than any of the true Chicagoans whom you have given to us, 'twice as natural' as life. . . ." This is an observation which doubtless caused Fuller considerable soul searching, and may well have played a part in his reply to a letter from Howells, some years later, in 1909 to be exact, urging him to write another Chicago novel, which Howells had suggested, half-jokingly no doubt, to repay him for his encouragement and critical advice:

> Yet, if I go to work to repay you, I shall have two permanent drawbacks to overcome: no great liking for the environment I must depict, and no great zest for life as it is lived. In such circumstances should a man write at all? . . . who, in a cheap and noisy time, wants 'fame'? To wish for consideration, and yet to shrink from celebrity—there is the modern paradox. I can't square it.
>
> All these conflicting considerations once adjusted, and the realistic Chicago novel of observation under way, what then? Who wants to read about this repellent town?

Fuller's problem in writing about Chicago may not have been so much his rejection of Chicago as the limitations of his own personality. His reticence, accentuated by his insecurity in dealing with women, could well have been the reason why having created such a strong and appealing character as Abby in *The Cliff-Dwellers* he was unable to bring her fully to life, and therefore abruptly ended the novel without really finishing the story. One has the impression that he felt as insecure in dealing with a character he had created, especially a woman, as with a real person. Jane and Mrs. Bates come out much better, for the reason, perhaps, that he could regard Jane, the sister of Truesdale, who was to some extent himself, as his own sister, and he develops Mrs. Bates entirely through the medium of Jane, thus making it unnecessary to encounter her himself. A novelist who finds it difficult to establish a close relationship with his own characters is obviously at a serious disadvantage, which may explain why Fuller, with the critical success his first four books had brought him and the support of the leading literary critic in the country, never seemed to realize, at least as a novelist, the full potential of his remarkable literary gifts. In the bibliography included in the authoritative study of Fuller by John Pilkington, Jr., eleven books are listed as having come from his hand following the publication of the first four, but none of them fulfills the promise implied in William Dean Howells' assertion in his review of *With the Procession*: "At present we have no one to compare with him in the East, in scale and quality of work."

In connection with all this it is interesting to observe that the one character in *The Cliff-Dwellers* that Fuller seems to realize fully is Cornelia McNabb, first met working behind the lunch counter in the Clifton. She is a straightforward, uncomplicated girl who has come from Pewaukee, Wisconsin, to "make it" in Chicago. As she explains one day to Ogden, whom she had first encountered when she was working as a waitress in the boarding house where he was living, "I'm going to get along, let me tell you. I haven't jumped on to this hobby-horse of a town just to stay still." She carefully studies the society pages of the Chicago newspapers to learn how the ladies at the top conduct themselves, and, after learning secretarial skills at night school, finds part-time work in small offices, which, in her practical way, she believes will lead to more promising opportunities than working in a single large office. Before long, she marries the son of Erastus Brainard, the owner of the bank in the Clifton.

Cornelia McNabb presented no problem to Fuller. She came from an entirely different background and wanted different things from life than he did. He no doubt had known such girls, from a safe distance, during the family summer vacations in Oconomowoc. He could bring her into the story and make her a convincing character without becoming involved in any way, even from the distance of a page in a book.

The book in which Fuller most clearly defines his artistic position and perhaps the best of his later work is *Under the Skylights*,
published in 1901. This is a witty satire of what he saw as the
artistic pretensions of Hamlin Garland and other members, including himself, of a group of writers, painters and sculptors known as
"The Little Room." They had begun to meet informally in the
studio of Lorado Taft at the time the preparations for the World's
Fair were first getting underway, and later moved to a room on the
top floor of the Fine Arts Building. The first, and perhaps the best
of the three stories that make up the book, "The Downfall of
Abner Joyce," is an amusing account of a young writer, originally
from a farm and a graduate of Flatfield Academy, newly arrived in
Chicago, who has made a name for himself with a collection of
stories describing the hardships of farm life, *This Weary World*.
He is an advocate of tax reform to equalize the burden between
the farmer and the city man, refuses at first even to associate with
anyone he suspects of having benefited from the "unearned increment," but is gradually corrupted by city life, and finally reaches
"an understanding with the children of Mammon. He—a great,
original genius—had become just like other people." In spite of
the clear identification of Abner Joyce with Hamlin Garland, it did
not disturb their friendship.

John Pilkington in his study of Henry Fuller follows his discussion of *Under the Skylights* with a somewhat different explanation
than suggested in the foregoing of Fuller's reasons for neglecting the
writing of novels in his later years:

> Beneath the comedy and the witticism of the three novelettes in
> *Under the Skylights*, Fuller was seriously defending his own artistic
> creed. Below his surface playfulness lay the whole long history of
> Fuller's quarrel with Chicago, his disappointment over the "up-
> ward movement," and his growing conviction that he was fighting
> a losing battle in defense of romance, idealism, and imagination as
> the essentials of art. If the art of the novelist was to become in the
> future merely the act of reporting, Fuller would withdraw from
> competition. His decision to withdraw becomes the salient fact of
> his career after 1900.

With this we come to the difficult, complex subject of Fuller's relations with Chicago. In the four large volumes of Hamlin Garland's reminiscences, which were based on his diaries, there are numerous references to his friend Henry B., from his pleasure at Fuller's acceptance of realism with the publication in 1893 of *The Cliff-Dwellers* to the understanding tribute to him written upon the news of his death in 1929. In many of these instances, Garland speaks of Fuller's dissatisfaction with his life in Chicago. The following is from a conversation with Fuller after Garland had told him of his decision to sell his comfortable Chicago house on a pleasant street near the University and move to New York, explaining that his livelihood depended entirely on the New York magazine and book publishers:

> "Why stay in this town if you can get out of it?" he demanded.
> "No writer can earn a living here except on the newspapers. If I
> could get away I would go to Italy and never return."

However strongly Fuller may have objected to Chicago, except for the year in Italy, the five or six subsequent trips to Italy and the year in Boston following the second sojourn abroad, he spent his life in Chicago. Whether he may have stayed in Boston had not the death of his father brought him back to Chicago there is no way of knowing, but for anyone as introverted as he was it would seem to have been difficult, if not impossible, to establish himself in a strange city, and life in Chicago had its compensations. He was well known and came from a respected family, there was his close friendship with Hamlin Garland who, with his family, must have provided a welcome refuge, and there were the weekly gatherings of The Little Room, which he seemed to enjoy and in which he took an active part. For a year or two, he had a weekly page for book reviews in the *Chicago Evening Post*, a much respected newspaper in those days, and in 1912 he took an active part with Harriet Monroe, whom he had known since his boyhood, in the launching of her *Poetry: A Magazine of Verse*. As Pilkington describes his part in this venture, "Although Fuller helped her to discover new talent and to establish the progressive, even revolutionary, reputation of the magazine, his most sustained contribution lay in his editorial abilities. . . . Fuller was an editor and proofreader without equal. Much of the excellence of *Poetry* was due to Fuller's high standards of writing and printing."

During the last years of his life he became a regular guest at the Sunday breakfasts of a University of Chicago professor, which often lasted the entire day. Another University professor, who had built an attractive house on top of one of the dunes on Lake Michigan south of Chicago, often invited him for the weekend. For all his longing for Italy, life in Chicago was not entirely empty.

While none of the books Fuller wrote after *Under the Skylights* seems to come up to the promise of the first four, he took an active part in the literary life of his time. In his reminiscences, Hamlin Garland speaks of him "As one of the wisest and keenest of my critics"; Thornton Wilder acknowledged his friendship and critical guidance, as did Louis Bromfield. Over the years, he contributed to many magazines, including *Harper's, Scribner's,* the *Atlantic, The Dial,* the *Nation,* the *New Republic* and the *New York Times.* During the four years of the *Freeman* under the editorship of Albert J. Nock, he contributed a book review every month, which was usually given the leading place. In her *History of the Freeman,* Susan J. Turner has this to say about Fuller's contribution to the literary excellence of that magazine:

> Fuller's reviews were bravura examples of the *Freeman*'s conservative side in letters. He brought to the magazine three decades of reading and writing experience, from the realism of Howells to the rediscovery of Henry James. He could compose a gracious and sympathetic account of Garland's autobiographies. . . . He could censure Cabell mildly for his social irresponsibility in a prose which was ornate, purple, and elegant; half a loving parody of Cabell, half akin to his own elegance.

As much as Fuller seemed to resent the fate that condemned him to spend his life in Chicago, there can be little doubt that he developed a degree of attachment to his native city and pride in the long association of his family with its history. He was a product of Chicago, as the character and specific quality of his work make clear, and with his high literary standards and unfailing critical judgment made his own contribution to its cultural life. At a time when Chicago was best known for its stockyards, it was Henry Fuller, as a young man in his thirties, who astonished the eastern reviewers by the quality of his writing.

Hamlin Garland: An Appreciation

A LTHOUGH LARGELY FORGOTTEN NOW, Hamlin Garland was a successful and much respected writer during the first quarter or so of this century. Of his some thirty published books, none is now in print, though one of them, his autobiographic *Son of the Middle Border*, went through numerous editions and was used in schools. He was not one of the great American writers, not a Melville, a Mark Twain, nor a Nathaniel Hawthorne, but he was an honest and competent author. His stories of the settlement of the West give an authentic account of what it was like, what it cost in human terms, both to those who lost their way of life, the Indians, and to those who gained a new beginning. He was there, he experienced it himself, and he tells it like it was.

Hamlin Garland was born in 1860 in LaCrosse, Wisconsin, then at the edge of settlement, what he liked to call the "middle border." His father came originally from Maine. In the excitement that swept the country following the discovery of gold in California, lured by the prospect of clear, open land, he left the security of family and of a close community to set out for the West. Garland tells this story, which in one form or another is part of the American Story, in *Trail-Makers of the Middle Border*. The story of his father's western migration includes his working as a lumberman in the forests of northern Wisconsin, driving log rafts down the Wisconsin River to the saw mills, and eventually settling on a 160-acre farm along the bluffs east of the Mississippi. On the day his father made the last payment on his farm he enlisted in the Union army,

Hamlin Garland

leaving his wife and three small children—Hamlin was the second—in the care of neighbors.

Garland's mother was of Scotch-Irish background and, as far as he knew, came from a family that had come to the Wisconsin frontier from Maryland. They were sturdy people. His McClintock grandmother, Garland tells us, had thirteen children, seven sons, of whom three were killed in the Civil War, and six daughters, all born in a crude Wisconsin cabin. He speaks of them all with great affection, of their love of music, of happy family gatherings, of his great, strong, dark-haired uncles who owned and always took charge of setting up the horse-driven machinery used in those days for thrashing. The first school he attended was in Onalaska, the destination of the log rafts that came down from the north to the saw mills on the islands in the river. "In the midst of this tumult, surrounded by this coarse, unthinking life, my Grandmother Garland's home stood, a serene small sanctuary of lofty womanhood, a temple of New England virtue."

Garland makes us feel that those years of his childhood were happy, filled with impressions that stayed with him for the rest of his life, but his father longed for the open land farther west—the rocky, hilly farm, which was all he could afford by the time he was in a position to buy land, reminded him too much of the New England farms he had left behind. When Garland was eight, his father sold the farm in Green's Coulee, as it was called, and set out for Iowa, but with a stop of a year or two on a farm in Minnesota. Garland describes the lure of the open land farther west—it was always farther west—to the Americans of his generation as only a man could who had experienced it in his own family. He tells of family gatherings when they sang what he calls "the fine old marching song" of the western migration which came from the crossing of the Alleghenies and begins

> *Cheer up, brothers, as we go*
> *O'er the mountains, westward ho—*
> *Where herds of deer and buffalo*
> *Furnish the fare.*

and ends with the jubilant chorus

> *Then o'er the hills in legions, boys,*
> *Fair freedom's star*
> *Points to the sunset regions, boys,*
> *Ha, ha, ha-ha—*

It wasn't great poetry, but as Garland says, when they sang it, his father's face "shone with the light of the explorer, the pioneer. The words of this song appealed to him as the finest poetry. It meant all that was fine and hopeful and buoyant in American life. . . ." Garland quotes his father, as an old man, telling him: "The best times I've ever had in my life was when I was cruising the prairie in a covered wagon."

It was a hard life to establish a home in a frontier community, particularly for the women, old before their time. Garland describes plowing the unbroken "dark, sandy loam" of Iowa while still a boy of ten for nine hours a day while his father was building a house to get a roof over their heads before winter, but there were compensations—the bountiful life of the wild prairie, the neighborliness of a frontier community with its square dances, barn raisings, thrashings—and it produced strong-willed, vigorous people, but for all that, Garland was never able to romanticize frontier life, he always saw it as his mother must have experienced it, as a never-ending round of demands on her strength and patience.

The family stayed twelve years in Iowa, long enough for Garland, rather against the will of his father, to attend and to finish what was called a "seminary" in the nearby town of Osage, which, with the training he had received in country schools, seems to have given him the rudiments of an education, and with its emphasis on oratory, helped him to gain self-confidence and to use words effectively. The school library, he said, was "pitifully small, consisting largely of Scott, Dickens, and Thackeray," but nosing about it in one day he discovered the two volumes of Hawthorne's *Mosses from an Old Manse*. "I turned a page or two and instantly my mental horizon widened. When I had finished the *Artist of the Beautiful*, the great Puritan romancer had laid his spell on me everlastingly. . . . The stately diction, the rich and glowing imagery, the mystical radiance, and the aloofness of the author's personality all united to create in me a worshipful admiration which made all other interests pale and faint." He also, he said, acquired a reading knowledge of French in that unpretentious Iowa "seminary." One cannot help wondering how many graduates of a modern high school go out into the world as well-prepared as he was.

After a disastrous crop failure or two, Garland's father sold his Iowa farm and pushed on to South Dakota which had recently been opened to settlement. A winter in South Dakota convinced Hamlin that pioneer life was not for him. After a year teaching in a country school back in Illinois, he made up his mind to get an education. He and his younger brother had spent a wonderfully broadening and stimulating summer in Boston and in wandering about the still unspoiled New England countryside, and having made their way by picking up jobs as they went along, he was confident of his ability to take care of himself. With three hundred dollars or so he had saved and the lure of Boston before him, the young Garland set out to make his way. How this raw farm boy from the prairies, arriving in Boston with only his three hundred dollars, knowing no one and with no connections, but with determination, a strong physique, and his native intelligence, managed to make himself a successful and respected author is an inspiring story. He calculated that by living on no more than five dollars a week he could last through the winter. Although his bare, small room was often cold and he could not afford a warm overcoat, and while he frequently went hungry, he managed to see many of the tragedies of Shakespeare played by Edwin Booth, which he would carefully study the next day in the library, to hear many of the great lecturers of the day—this was the era of the lecture—to attend concerts of the Boston Symphony, for which a gallery seat then cost 25¢, and to spend many satisfying hours in the public library. Harvard, which he had hoped for, proved to be out of reach. For a young man with a receptive mind and anxious to learn, all this, discouraging as it must have been, was a greatly fulfilling experience, and Garland made the most of it.

Edwin Booth taught me the power and the glory of English speech. He made me feel very rude and small and poor, but he inspired me.

> He aroused my ambition. . . . Booth and his Shakespeare were the greatest educative experiences in my life at this time. Outwardly seedy, hungry, pale and lonely, I inhabited palaces and spoke with kings.

With the arrival of spring, his money almost gone, pale and gaunt as was fitting for an aspiring poet living in a garret, his fortunes suddenly took a turn for the better when, following a lecture, he went up to speak to Moses True Brown, the head of the Boston School of Oratory. Brown was impressed by this serious, intense young man and invited him to come to talk to him. This was followed by an invitation to attend classes without charge and, after a few months, to give lectures as "Professor Garland," for which he was paid a small stipend. A public lecture, "Edwin Booth as Iago," caught the attention of a prominent Boston lady who invited him to give a series of lectures in her stately house, for which she charged admission and dragooned her friends into attending. Garland netted ninety dollars from these lectures, a princely sum for him. He also met the literary editor of the *Boston Transcript*, who invited him to review books, one review of William Dean Howells' *The Minister's Charge* subsequently led to a meeting with the great man himself, winning his support and friendship. Garland made his first literary sale at this time, a "long poem of the prairies," as he described it, to *Harper's Weekly*, which netted him twenty-five dollars, with which he bought a piece of silk for his mother and *The Memoirs of General Grant* for his father.

It was during this time that Garland began to realize that as much as he loved Boston and New England and as grateful as he was for all they had done for him, his proper subject was the "warm, broad, unkempt and tumultuous West." In his first article, therefore, he set out to describe a typical scene from Middle Western farm life as he had known it. This was *The Western Corn Husking*, which he sent to the *New American Magazine*. Almost by return mail he received an encouraging letter from the editor who asked for more such articles. Garland set to work at once, taking up the seasons, one by one. The magazine didn't pay much, but Garland was now a published author. Having saved enough to visit his family, about one hundred dollars, he says, he set off after the end of the spring term, first to visit friends in Osage, Iowa, where he had gone to school, and then on to South Dakota to see his family. On the way he stopped in Chicago to call on Joseph Kirkland, a prominent lawyer, who had responded to Garland's review in the *Boston Transcript* of his novel, *Zury*, with an invitation to come to see him. Kirkland confirmed Garland's growing conviction that middle western farm life was his proper subject. When Hamlin reached his father's farm in South Dakota, the harvest was just beginning. He asked his father to hire him as a regular hand on the thrashing crew, not only because he needed the money, but more than that, to experience again what farm work was really like, having in mind Kirkland's admonition to write about farm life as it was. At the end of the week, he tells us, he wrote to his friend Kirkland in Chicago and enclosed some of the detailed notes he had written down, and heard in reply, "You're the first actual farmer in American fiction— now tell the truth about it."

Garland left his family taking with him a story his mother had told him. Written down and later published, this story, *Mrs. Ripley's Trip*, was one of his best. It was after his return to Boston, still under the weight of the contrast between the beauty and abundance of the countryside and the drabness of the lives of those who farmed it, that he heard a lecture by Henry George. In consequence of all these impressions, he "joined the anti-poverty brigade," as he described it, became a single-taxer, gave speeches for the populist cause, and bent down to his writing "with a fierce resolve." This resulted in a number of sketches and stories that set out to present life on a middle western farm as it was. The first of these, *A Prairie Heroine*, a study of a crisis in the life of a despairing farm woman, he sent to the *Arena*, a new magazine published in Boston which, because it treated the populist movement with some sympathy, was regarded as radical. To Garland's delight, the *Arena* accepted the article at once, and the editor, B. O. Flower, encouraged him to continue along the same lines. In 1891, the Arena Publishing Company brought out six of these sketches and stories under the title, *Main-Travelled Roads*, Garland's first book. Critics, especially in the West, who preferred to see farm life in a more romantic light than the realistic Garland, were mostly critical, but William Dean Howells, one of the most respected literary critics of the day, devoted a large part of his regular page in *Harper's* to its defense, and Walt Whitman, Garland says, hailed him as one of the literary pioneers of the West, for whom the poet said he had been waiting. Garland had made his way and now felt sufficiently established as a writer to give up his job at the Boston School of Oratory.

Garland seems to have been as restless as his father. He travelled about Kansas and Nebraska giving speeches for the populist cause and gathering material for a longer article on the subject for the *Arena*. He and his younger brother, who had become a successful actor, settled for a time in New York. But in 1892 he was attracted to Chicago by the creative ferment and excitement aroused by the preparation for the 1893 World's Fair. After several visits, which gave him the opportunity to meet a number of writers and publishers, all under the spell, as he was, of the prospect of Chicago becoming a great literary and cultural center, he rented rooms in 1893 on Elm Street, not far from the lake, and soon became very much a part of the city. Writing about all this thirty years later in his book of reminiscence, *Roadside Meetings*, he has this to say about Chicago as it was then:

> As I look back on it now, I can see that it was only a big country trade center containing less than a million people, an ugly, smoky, muddy town built largely of wood and without a single beautiful structure. Its great men were sons of villagers, its university only a few mean buildings.

Garland arranged to have three books published by two of the new Chicago publishers, *Prairie Songs* and a new edition of *Main-Travelled Roads* by Stone & Kimball and *Prairie Folks* by Francis Schulte. He and Herbert Stone became good friends, but Stone, who delighted in beautifully produced books, brought out Garland's books in such an elegant fashion that they were too high priced to sell, which did not, of course, please the author, and Francis Schulte soon went bankrupt, all of which confirmed Garland's conviction that when he expressed the belief, after first arriving in Chicago, that it was "about to take its place among the literary capitals of the world," he had been mistaken.

Not long after Garland had settled in Chicago, Franklin Head, a leading merchant and prominent in the cultural life of the city, invited him to give a lecture in his elegant home on the near north side on "Impressionism in Art," a controversial subject in those days. It was following this lecture that Garland met the sculptor Lorado Taft, the beginning of a long friendship, one consequence of which was Garland's marriage in 1899, after a long courtship, to Taft's sister, Zulime.

Lorado Taft, as his work testifies, was a gifted, creative artist and, from all accounts, also an outgoing, genial man. His large studio, then on Van Buren Street, by the time Garland met him had become a gathering place for young artists and writers, a group which Garland soon joined. They later met in a studio of one of the artists in the Fine Arts Building, and the group took on the name "The Little Room," from the name of an intermittently vanishing chamber in a contemporary story by Madelaine Yale Wynne. The creative euphoria that had swept Chicago with the 1893 World's Fair soon ebbed away and "the city fell back into something like its former drabness of business enterprise," as Garland was later to write in his book, *Roadside Meetings*. The new publishing firms launched a few years before with so much hope and enthusiasm, Way & Williams, Francis Schulte, Stone & Kimball, later to become Herbert S. Stone & Co., by 1905 were all gone. *The Chap-Book*, the "little" magazine of Stone & Kimball which had launched the esthetic revolt of the 1890s, the "revolution in pianissimo" as Mencken called it, had already succumbed before the approaching twentieth century. In trying to explain why Chicago, contrary to his expectations, was unable to support an active literary life of its own, why its authors left the city, Garland was later to write, "Because there are few supporters of workers in the fine arts. Western men do not think in terms of art. . . . Until Chicago has at least one magazine founded like a university, and publishing houses like Scribners and Macmillan our authors and artists must go to New York."

It was during those first years in Chicago that Garland, from having been a crusading reformer for the single tax and justice for the farmer, became a successful, rather conventional writer. Instead of writing for the *Arena*, he now wrote for the *Ladies Home Journal* and *Collier's*. A successful book of his during those years was *The Life of General Grant*, which he wrote at the suggestion of S. S. McClure. It was first serialized in *McClure's* magazine and then published as a book in 1899. The transformation of Garland from ardent reformer to successful writer, for which he has been sharply criticized as having sacrificed his ideals, is amusingly described, as we have seen, by his friend Henry Fuller in *The Downfall of Abner Joyce*, part of the book *Under the Skylights* (*1901*). Abner, in Fuller's satire, arrives in Chicago from a downstate farm, having "taken a place" in literature, as Fuller puts it, with his book *This Weary World* which "was grim and it was rugged, but it was sincere and it was significant." Fuller goes on to say, "Abner's book comprised a dozen short stories—twelve clods of earth gathered, as it were, from the very field across which he himself, a farm boy, had once guided the plow. . . . Some of the stories seemed written not so much by the hand as by the fist, a fist quivering from the tension of muscles and sinews fully ready to act for truth and right." He was invited to join a group of writers and artists who met together from time to time and was gradually lured away from the friends he had been associating with, distributing pamphlets and giving lecturers on Sunday afternoons to small and dwindling audiences on the "Readjusted Tax." At one of his first meetings with his new friends, a genial member who, Abner discovers, has been favored to an "exceptional degree by that monster of inconsistency and injustice, the Unearned Increment," invited him to lunch at his club. " 'Club'—fatal word; it chilled Abner in a second. He knew about clubs! Clubs were the places where the profligate children of Privilege drank improper drinks and told improper stories and kept improper hours. . . ." Abner, of course, declined, but he gradually gave in to the blandishments of what he felt to be "a sort of decorous Bohemia and to feel that such, after all, was the atmosphere he had been really destined to breathe." He soon found himself joining them almost every Saturday afternoon, and on one such occasion Mrs. Palmer Pence, the great lady in those days of Chicago . . . "a robust and vigorous woman in her prime," as Fuller describes her "... handsome and rich and intelligent and ambitious," joined the group, and noticing Abner, asked to be introduced to him. "Confronted by his stalwart limbs and expansive shoulders, she was no longer a behemoth—she felt almost like a sylph. She looked up frankly, and with a sense of growing comfort, into his broad face where a strong growth of chestnut beard was bursting through his ruddy cheeks and swirling abundantly beneath his nose. She looked up higher, to his wide forehead, where a big shock of confident hair rolled and tumbled about in careless affluence. And with no great shyness she appraised his hands and his feet—those strong forceful hands that had dominated the lurching, self-willed plough, those sturdy feet that had resolutely tramped the miles of bumpy furrow the ploughshare had turned up blackly to the sun and air. She shrank, she dwindled. Her slender girlhood— that remote, incredible time—was on her once more."

Making the appropriate allowances for the exaggeration implied in such a satire, Hamlin Garland, in the guise of Abner Joyce, seems to have appeared to Chicago much like Abner Joyce when he first arrived on the scene. From all accounts, he was a vigorous, outgoing, striking-looking man, which is demonstrated by the fact that he was able to win the hand of the beautiful and talented Zulime Taft.

With his modest earnings from lecturing and writing, Garland was able to buy a house in West Salem, Wisconsin, near his birthplace for his father and mother, who were still living on the farm Garland had left to make his way to Boston. His father resisted; pioneer that he was, he still dreamed of moving farther west to irrigated land, but they finally lived happily on the place their son had provided for them, and it later became a much loved summer place for his family. During the years before his marriage, Garland spent many weeks in the summer riding in the Rockies, visiting Indian camps, talking with prospectors, gathering material for stories and articles. He often went alone, but in the summer of 1895 he invited two artists friends from Chicago who had never been west of the Mississippi to go with him, Charles Francis Brown, a landscape painter, and Hermon MacNeill, a sculptor, in search of material in Colorado and Arizona. Leaving his friends one day in Cripple

Creek, then at the height of its fame as a mining camp, Garland set off to find a roundup. Garland's account of his experiences will give some impression of his skill in describing what life in the West was like in those days:

> As we are eating breakfast the next morning, everybody feeling damp and stiff in the joints, we heard the dull throbbing of hoofs, and down the valley came the horse wrangler, shouting, a troop of horses rushing wildly before him.
>
> The wrangler rounded the drove toward the tents, whence issued the riders, lariats in hand. The horses were all broncos, small, alert, flat-limbed, wide-eyed, and tricky, and had to be caught with the rope. The men surrounded them, herding them into a compact squad. The riders advanced into the herd one by one, with coiled ropes ready, and nosed and pulled out their best horses, for the ride was to be hard. At last all were secured, the riders swung into their saddles and dashed away with that singular, swift-gliding, sidewise gallop so characteristic of these men and their ponies, off for some seven hours of the hardest riding in a blinding fog and a thick-falling rain.

On a later riding trip to the mountains, Garland ran into an old schoolfriend from Iowa, who had started out studying theology and ended up a "mountain man." At the time the country had been electrified by the news of the discovery of gold in the Klondike and Garland's friend urged him to go to Alaska with him. "He was a veritable gold seeker, whereas I was merely seeking adventure and a more advanced schooling in the art of the trailer," Garland later wrote in *Roadside Meetings*. On April 19, 1898 he left West Salem for the town in British Columbia which was the starting place for the trek to the Klondike. There he bought the horse that saw him through and which he managed to ship back to West Salem.

> I had been gone a little over five months. I had no gold to show and to bring my horse out with me had cost over a thousand dollars; but I was rich in knowledge. I had served a severe apprenticeship. "No one can tell me anything about riding the trail," I said to my friends. "I am now a master trailer."

While he was not to be rewarded with gold for his efforts, *Mc-Clure's Magazine* bought the Klondike poems he had written in the saddle or around campfires, and a book came out of it, *The Long Trail, A Story of the Northwest Wilderness*, which appeared originally in *The Youth's Companion*.

In 1907, Garland was able to buy a comfortable, three-story house in Woodlawn, on the south side of Chicago, not far from the University, where he lived with his wife and two daughters until he and his family moved to New York in 1915. As indicated earlier, Garland seemed a restless man, was often away giving lectures, an important source of income, or visiting his publishers in New York or Philadelphia; besides all this, the mountain country of the West still had a strong attraction for him. But judging from his various reminiscences, he particularly enjoyed taking part in the literary life of New York. He was an active member of the Players Club, which had been founded in the 1890s in the former house of Edwin Booth on Gramercy Park, and later became a member of the Century Club; he also maintained his close relations with William Dean Howells, who by then was living in New York, and he seems to have been a welcome addition to any group of writers or publishers. In his account in *Roadside Meetings* of a stay in New York around 1900 he speaks of running into Stephen Crane, who was an old friend, at a gathering of some kind; of his first meeting with Booth Tarkington; of being invited by Rudyard Kipling to come to see him in the company of Israel Zangwill, which was followed by a dinner with Kipling and James Whitcomb Riley; of renewing his friendship with John Burroughs; of a stimulating lunch with George Brett, the head of Macmillan, in the Century Club; of spending the night in the palatial home of Cyrus Curtis of the Curtis Publishing Company in Philadelphia; and of receiving an invitation from Henry James to visit him in Rye—all rather heady stuff for a farm boy from the prairies.

In spite of his awareness of the deficiencies of Chicago as a literary center and his disappointment at the collapse of the two Chicago publishers to whom he had entrusted several of his books and for whom he had had high hopes, Garland was determined to do what he could to make Chicago a more stimulating place for artists and writers. The group who met in The Little Room seems to have convinced him that, as he reports having remarked one day to his brother-in-law Lorado Taft, "the time has come when a successful literary and artistic club can be established and maintained." He discussed the idea with several other members of The Little Room, including Henry Fuller, Charles Francis Browne, and Ralph Clarkson. All were in favor except Henry Fuller who, in spite of, or perhaps because of, the fact that he was third-generation Chicago, took a dim view of the prospects of Chicago as a cultural center. According to Garland, Fuller regarded the city as "a pestilential slough in which he was inextricably mired," and would never join, although the title of one of his novels, *The Cliff-Dwellers*, provided the name for the club. After a number of meetings, Garland was able to enlist the support of such influential men as Charles Hutchinson, Howard Van Doren Shaw, Frederick Stock, Francis Hackett, Paul Shorey, and Frederick C. Bartlett, among others, and on January 6, 1909, with appropriate ceremony, the club now ensconced in the penthouse on the top of Orchestra Hall was inaugurated.

Garland became the first president and, largely through his efforts and the standing he enjoyed as a much respected and successful writer, was able to make the Cliff Dwellers the center of cultural life he had hoped for. But the membership was apparently not quite ready for the rather austere club that President Garland had in mind: no alcoholic drinks of any kind were permitted, conversation at the table was to be on a high order, discussion of business and business lunches were frowned on, and frequently a visiting prominent writer or artist was invited to speak. In consequence of all this, and particularly of the ban on alcohol in any form, on January 15, 1919 Charles Hutchinson was elected president to succeed Hamlin Garland. His rather abrupt dismissal as president of the club he had founded doubtless hurt Garland, but it probably also came as a release: it provided the push to leave Chicago and move to New York, which he had realized for some time was necessary for his career as a writer. He quotes his friend Henry Fuller as remarking to him, after a discussion of the subject: "Why stay in this town if you can get out of it? No writer can earn a living here except on the newspapers." Garland goes on to say in one of his books of literary reminiscence, *My Friendly Contemporaries*:

> Not one dollar of my income came from Western publishers and it
> was always with a sense of weakness and dismay that I reentered
> Chicago from New York. . . . It may be counted as a weakness, but
> I was no longer content to live the life of a literary pioneer. I came
> to Chicago in 1893, at the time of the great Columbian Exposition,
> and I had aided, in so far as I could, to build up the esthetic and
> literary side of the city's life.

He sold his Woodlawn house in 1915 and took his family to live in a New York apartment, without regret, it would seem: "For twenty-three winters, I had endured the harsh winds of Chicago, and fought against its ugliness, now I was free of it."

More than fifty years after Garland's death, and having come to know him slightly as a man, what are we to say of his work as a writer? Garland's first book, *Main-Travelled Roads*, was written at the time of his commitment to what he later called "the anti-poverty brigade," justice for the farmer, Henry George's single tax, and under the impression of his recent visit to his parents, still struggling on the bleak farm in South Dakota. The original edition included six stories, which were given a degree of continuity by an introductory sentence following each title. The second, *Up the Coulé*, in its intensity and theme is characteristic of the book as a whole. It tells the story of the visit of an older brother, who has gone to the city and become a successful and rich actor, to his brother who has stayed on the farm. It opens with the impression made by the bountiful, well-cultivated Wisconsin countryside as seen from a train window on a fine summer day.

Arriving in the small town he had left ten years before, the actor brother finds it as unprepossessing as ever. An old acquaintance offers to take him in his wagon to his brother's farm, a trip that brings back many memories. He appreciates as never before the quiet beauty and evening fragrance of the valley as they drive into the hills to the farm. The impression of his brother's farm is quite different: ". . . a small white house, story-and-a-half structure, with a wing, set in the midst of a few locusts; a small drab-colored barn, with a sagging ridge pole; a barnyard full of mud in which a few cows were standing, fighting the flies and waiting to be milked. An old man was pumping water at the well; the pigs were squealing from a pen nearby; a child was crying."

It was not a happy visit. The younger brother has struggled manfully to pay off the mortgage he had inherited with the family farm, but has finally lost that farm and is now on another, poorer farm, their mother is incapacitated from the hard work of a farmer's wife, and both the brother and his wife, a former teacher, are thoroughly dissatisfied with the life they feel they are forced to lead. The story ends:

> The two men stood there, face to face, hands clasped, the one
> fair-skinned, full-lipped, handsome in his neat suit; the other
> tragic, somber in his softened mood, his large, long, rugged Scotch
> face bronzed with sun and scarred with wrinkles that had histories,
> like sabre-cuts on a veteran, the record of his battles.

A touching, less bitter story, which ends the book, is *Mrs. Ripley's Trip*—this is the story, in somewhat expanded form, that his mother had told him during his visit to their South Dakota farm. For twenty-three years Mrs. Ripley had uncomplainingly taken care of her family and done the work of a farmer's wife. Now she announces to her incredulous husband that she plans to visit her relatives in New York State, which she left as a girl.

"Howgy 'xpect to get the money, mother? Anybody died and left yeh a pile?"

"Never you mind where I get the money, so's 't *you* don't haff to bear it. The land knows if I'd 'a' waited for *you* to pay my way—"

He is shamed into selling two shoats to raise the money, but to his amazement she already has it, carefully saved over the years for the purpose and stored in a woolen sock.

Before leaving, she has baked several mince pies, fried up a batch of doughnuts, killed and boiled a chicken, made up pancake batter and left instructions for her husband and grandson, Tewsbury, who lives with them. When she comes back, "Tukey," as they call him, is building a fire in the stove. He rushes to greet her with the welcome news, "Oh, gran'ma, I'm so glad to see you! We had an awful time since you've been gone." The kitchen is a mess, dirty dishes piled up and the stove covered with pancake batter. By the time her husband, Ripley, as she calls him, comes in from the barn, she has cleaned up the kitchen and is elbow deep in the dishpan. The story has a perfect, appropriate ending:

"Hullo, mother! Got back, hev yeh?"

"I sh'd say it was about time," she replied briefly, without looking up or ceasing work. "Has ol' 'Crumpy' dried up yet?" This was her greeting.

Her trip was a fact now; no chance could rob her of it. She had looked forward twenty-three years toward it, and now she could look back at it accomplished. She took up her burden again, never more thinking to lay it down.

Contrary to most of the farm women in Garland's stories, Mrs. Ripley is contented. She may not be radiantly happy as happiness is understood these days, but she has met the demands of life and carried her burden without complaint; she is content. She and her husband, as both well know, however little they may show it, are dependent on each other and are real people, as the actor and the farmer and his wife are not—they are caricatures, made to fit the point of the story, the contrast between the successful city man and the struggling farmer.

Mrs. Ripley's Trip is a good story, skillfully told, makes a valid point, and is a pleasure to read. Except for the *Return of the Private*, which is based on Garland's memory of his father coming back from the war, the other stories in *Main-Travelled Roads* all suffered from the same fault as *Up the Coulé*, the characters and the stories themselves are made to fit Garland's purpose in writing them. There are two novels from Garland's "anti-poverty" period, both published by Arena, *Jason Edwards* and *A Spoil of Office*. They attracted some attention as populist tracts and doubtless served a useful purpose in doing so, but in selecting books for a new edition of his work to be published by Harpers in 1924 he rejected them both. *Jason Edwards*, he wrote in *My Friendly Contemporaries*, ". . . is too short, too sour of temper, too drab of color, too preachy." *A Spoil of Office* was discarded because its "characters are too largely political reformers." But in the introduction for a new edition of *Main-Travelled Roads* written in 1922, Garland, referring to this book and the above two novels, remarks, "If they seem unduly austere, let the reader remember the time in which they were composed. That they were true of the farms of that day no one can know better than I, for I was there—a Farmer."

When Garland returned from his excursion to the Klondike he said, "Henceforth I am the novelist." His populist, reforming days were past. One of the first results of this decision was the novel *The Captain of the Gray-Horse Troop*, which was serialized in the *Ladies Home Journal* in 1901 and published as a book the following year. In considering his books for the 1922 Harper edition, he mentions this as his most successful novel. One can say with some confidence that it is not one of the great novels, the story, in fact, is somewhat reminiscent of the cowboy and Indian movies offered on Saturday afternoon years ago for 10¢, but for all that, the picture it gives of Indian life is authentic and deeply felt. The main character is an army captain who, as the government agent on a reservation, is fighting off the attempts of ranchers and mining interests to steal the Indians' land. An attractive young lady, the daughter of a wealthy U.S. senator who represents the mining interests, comes to the reservation to paint the Indians. In trying to explain to her why her picture of an old Indian, Crawling Elk, doesn't truly represent him, the captain tells her:

> Crawling Elk is the annalist and storyteller of his tribe. He carries the 'winter count' and the sacred pipe, and can tell you of every movement of the Tetongs for more than a century and a half. His mind is full of poetry, and his conceptions of the earth and sky are beautiful. He knows little that the white men know, and cares for very little what the white man fights for, but his mind teems with the lore of the mysterious universe into which he has been thrust, and which he has studied for seventy-two years.

All this and the picture it gives of the mountain country make the book worth reading. The description of a mountain boy on a horse is particularly striking and makes it apparent that Garland was himself a horseman: "The boy made a fine figure as he swept past them with the speed of an eagle. His was the perfection of range horsemanship. He talked, gesticulated, rolled cigarettes, put his coat on or off as he rode, with no apparent thought of his horse or of the ground he crossed."

His most widely read book and perhaps his best, for which he won the Pulitzer Prize, is *Son of the Middle Border*, which takes the story of his life to the purchase of the house in Wisconsin for his parents. Besides the two mentioned, he wrote two other "Middle Border" books—*Daughter of the Middle Border* and *Back-Trailers of the Middle Border*. The first is centered around his mother, his wife and his two daughters, and takes his story from his marriage in 1899 to the death of his father. *Back-Trailers* is concerned with his return to the East, his desertion, so to speak, of the West, and is probably the weakest of the four. But *Son of the Middle Border* is a true-to-life account of the settlement of the West and will live as a contribution of American history. Even H. L. Mencken, a cocky city boy if there ever was one, who isn't willing to give Garland credit for much, reluctantly concedes: "It is, in substance, a document of considerable value—a naive and often highly illuminating contribution to the history of the American peasantry. . . . It is an honest book. There is some bragging in it, of course, but not much. It tells an interesting story. It radiates hard effort and earnest purpose."

If Garland thought *Captain of the Gray-Horse Troop* his most successful and perhaps his best, so be it. As for his books on spiritualism, a subject he became interested in to the point of attending seances, perhaps no opinion is required. As a professional writer, dependent on his pen to support his family, Garland was compelled to write what would sell. One can honestly say, then, with no disrespect intended for their author, that his novels and magazine articles fit the category of "pot-boilers." If the *Gray-Horse Troop*, however, is a good example of his novels, it is a tribute to his integrity as an author that it tells a good story and after three generations is still worth reading.

When Garland met with the editors of Harpers to work out a new edition of his work, it was suggested that his Indian stories be collected in one large volume and brought out in a rather elaborate edition with illustrations by Frederick Remington, many of them in color. Garland, however, didn't care for Remington's work, which he felt completely misrepresented the Indian, and was concerned that the resulting price, six dollars (the equivalent of fifty dollars today) would kill its sale. *The Book of the American Indian*, as it turned out, is a handsome book in a large format, and in spite of Garland's fears that it was too expensive to sell, went through a number of printings and is now a collector's item. Garland had become familiar with Indians in his boyhood, frequently running into them on his pack trips in the mountains, and he understood and appreciated them. In 1900 or thereabouts, he is often not specific about dates, he spent a summer in the Sioux country "having in mind," as he wrote later, "a plan to write some sort of story of Sitting Bull." The Sioux, as it happened, were assembled for "The White Man's Big Sunday," as they called the Fourth of July celebration, which included dances and a mimic battle, five thousand of them encamped in a big circle. With the help of two Indian traders who spoke Sioux fluently and enjoyed their confidence, Garland spent many days gathering stories and material from the Sioux who had been associated with their great chief, including the older man named Slohan, who had been a member of Sitting Bull's council of advisors, "The Silent Eaters," as they were called. The following from *Companions of the Trail*, one of the four books of reminiscences Garland later wrote, will give some conception of what went into the Indian book:

> All that afternoon—a witheringly hot day—we sat in the shade of the cabin and talked of the "Silent Eaters," of Sitting Bull, of the Ghost Dances, of the ancient history of the Sioux, and as we talked, Slohan grew in stature. He was essentially the poet, the dramatist. His gestures, in accompaniment to his speech, were magnificently picturesque and graphic. He forgot his grief as he forgot his present. He was no longer the poor, ragged, lonely old prisoner in the wan land of the white man; he was a councilor of his great chief, the chosen leader of the tribe, the Sioux of the plains.

The last half of *The Book of the American Indian* is made up of Garland's story of Sitting Bull and has the title *The Silent Eaters*.

It is Garland at his best. His account of the confrontation of the chief of the Sioux with General Miles is tragic drama of a high order: the Indian, fleeing in the middle of a cruel winter with his people before the U. S. Army, but determined that they would "live as the Great Spirit ordained that they should," and the implacable soldier, equally determined that "they must submit and come under the rule of Washington." Garland was an attentive listener, had a good memory, and great skill in bringing the material he had gathered into a coherent and convincing story, and nowhere is this skill put to better use than in *The Silent Eaters*.

During his long ride to Alaska, Garland made up his mind that henceforth he would keep an accurate daily record of the people he met, of what they talked about, and of his impressions. Discussing his literary plans many years later, in 1928, with George Brett, the head of Macmillan, who had published his "Middle Border" books, the publisher asked him what he planned to do with the diaries that resulted from all those conversations. After much discussion, Brett told him: "Your diaries are, in effect, a panoramic history of American art and letters over the past forty years. Why not write for us a literary biography, a volume dealing wholly with your experience as a writer? I think such a volume can be made the most important book of your life." When Garland interjected that there were thirty volumes of his diaries, Brett told him "he didn't care how many volumes you sent to us. This work should be your final and crowning contribution to American literature." Out of this suggestion four volumes appeared, handsomely produced in a uniform edition: *Companions of the Trail* in 1929, *Roadside Meetings* in 1930, *My Friendly Companions* in 1932, and *Afternoon Neighbors* in 1934. While they are not the sort of books many would sit down and read from cover to cover, they are full of rewarding accounts of the many literary figures Garland in his long and rich life came to know: a weekend in Rye with Henry James; Joaquin Miller, the "poet of the Sierras," in Chicago, which brings back a vanished and colorful era of American history; conversations in England with Joseph Conrad; a visit to Edith Wharton in her elegant house in the South of France; a pilgrimage, one might call it, as a young man, to Walt Whitman, a frail, old man, then living in a tenement in Camden, New Jersey, but

Theodore Dreiser

immaculate in his snowy white hair and beard. That was his final large effort, a fitting end to the work of a truly American writer.

Despite this rather rambling account of Hamlin Garland's life and work, it should nevertheless be clear that he is an American writer who deserves to be remembered. He was not blessed, it seems evident, with an imagination that extended much beyond his immediate experience nor with what might be called an exuberant sense of humor, but he understood his Middle Border characters, had a keen ear for their manner of speech, and recounted it all honestly. As has been observed, he was a restless man, like his father, never satisfied really wherever he happened to be, which may be one of the reasons for his fascination with the Indian, who, in his primitive state, Garland believed, accepted the world as it was given to him without the compelling urge to change it. In his Indian book, Garland recounts a conversation with an old Sioux who, after describing their life before the arrival of the white man, concludes:

> You would look long to find a people as happy as we were, because we lived as the Great Spirit had taught us to do, with no thought of change.

It is fitting that this son of American pioneers who were always pushing on "to the sunset regions," should have died, at the age of eighty, in California, the end of the westward trail.

Theodore Dreiser: A Great Writer in Spite of Himself

IN THE SUMMER OF 1887, with the blessing of his mother and six dollars in his pocket, Theodore Dreiser, having reached the age of sixteen, took the afternoon train from Warsaw, Indiana, for Chicago, three hours away, determined to make his way in the world. His family, pursued, as it must have seemed, by misfortune and poverty, had moved from one Indiana town to another. Before

Warsaw, there had been Terre Haute, Evansville, Sullivan, and even for a few months, Chicago. Difficult as his boyhood must have been, in his book devoted to Indiana, *A Hoosier Holiday*, Dreiser recalls those boyhood years with affection. He describes staring out the kitchen window early on a summer day:

> The boy looks at the sky. He loves the feel of the dawn. He knows nothing of whence he is coming or where he is going, only all is sensuously, deliriously gay and beautiful; youth is his; the tingle and response of a new body; the bloom and fragrance of the clover is in the air; the sense of the mystery of flying. He sits and sings some tuneless song. Of such is the kingdom of heaven.

The father of the family, John Dreiser, was born in 1821 in Mayen, a town of Roman origin in the Eifel hills of Germany, north of the Mosel and west of the Rhine. Mayen is noted for its mill wheels, made from the hard volcanic rock of the region, for the tenaciousness of its inhabitants, and for its rich tradition for folk tales. John Dreiser, who came to American in 1844, is described as industrious, ambitious, strong-willed and militantly Catholic. He was a weaver by trade and, having worked successfully in several places, decided to start his own woolen mill. After getting the necessary equipment and stock of wool, his mill was destroyed by fire and, having no insurance, he was burdened with debt for much of his life. It was this misfortune that determined the circumstances of his family. The mother of the family, born Sarah Maria Schänäb, came from a prosperous Mennonite farm family who disowned their daughter for marrying a Catholic. "My mother, a dreamy, poetic, impractical soul," as her son Theodore described her, "was serving to the best of her ability as the captain of the family ship." She raised ten children, of whom Theodore was the ninth. Dreiser's older brother, Paul, who used the name Dresser, became a successful actor and wrote more than a hundred popular songs, many of them very successful—*On the Banks of the Wabash, My Mother Told Me So, The Letter that Never Came*. During his periods of intermittent prosperity, Paul came to the rescue of the struggling family on a number of occasions, and when his novelist brother was going through a severe depression brought on by the suppression of his first novel, stepped in and quite literally saved his life. It was a family that ran to extremes, as might be expected from parents so sharply different in background and temperament—one from an uncomplicated Mennonite farm family, the other an intense, strong-willed Catholic from the German Rhineland.

Dreiser was not a Chicago writer in the sense that Henry Fuller was, but he grew up in the shadow of Chicago, discovered his talent for writing by working on a Chicago newspaper, and it was Chicago that gave him the inspiration and setting for his first novel, *Sister Carrie*. One of Dreiser's most powerful novels—H. L. Mencken considered it among his best—*The Titan*, takes place in Chicago during the time of the great traction tycoon, Charles Yerkes. No other writer has described the passion for money and power, the political corruption and the financial chicanery that characterized Chicago during the 1880s and 1890s more vividly than Dreiser. If he was not completely a native of Chicago, still he surely knew and understood the city.

Coming to the great, driving city on the shore of Lake Michigan which seemed to offer so much promise, the boy from a small town in Indiana dreamed of working in an elegant haberdashery shop or in a well-appointed office—he was inclined to such dreams—but soon came face to face with the reality of a great metropolis. After many rebuffs he finally found a job as dishwasher in a cheap restaurant on Halsted Street at $5 a week plus lunch. After losing various jobs, he was awkward, inexperienced, and not strong enough for hard physical labor, Dreiser was found by a former teacher from Warsaw who had recognized his talent and befriended him, and who now offered to send him, at her expense, to Indiana University. He accepted, but stayed only for one year. After returning to Chicago, by sheer persistence he was able to get himself hired as a reporter for the *Chicago Globe* with instructions "to cover the hotels for political news." He knew nothing about politics or how to write a news story, but more important than that, he was resourceful, observant and imaginative. His managing editor was helpful, if also ruthless with his copy, and one day remarked to him, "You know, Theodore, you have your faults, but you do know how to observe." It was then that he discovered that he loved to write.

Dreiser's career, like that of many writers, began as a newspaper-man.

The next step in Dreiser's apprenticeship was the *St. Louis Globe-Democrat*. While in St. Louis he met and fell madly in love—it was never difficult for Dreiser to fall madly in love—with Sara Osborne White, a pretty Missouri farm girl, but after meeting her younger sister wished he had waited for her. According to his biographer, W. A. Swanberg, he had planned "a quick seduction," later admitting that it was "her charming physical self that I craved." When she resisted he asked her, rather against his will, because he didn't wish to be tied down, to marry him, which he finally managed, under pressure, some six years later. It is characteristic of Dreiser that he blamed the eventual failure of his marriage to this loyal, patient woman, not on his numerous and flagrant infidelities, but on "the formalities, traditions, beliefs of a conventional and puritanic region." In the midst of the frustrations associated with the "puritanical" Sara White, his uninhibited brother Paul appeared in St. Louis with his theatrical company. Paul, who seemed to recognize the genius of his brother, urged him to come to New York. He also advised him to wait before marrying Sara White, which he was too poor to do anyway. Not having sufficient confidence to face the challenge of New York, all this only increased Dreiser's restlessness. He left the *Globe-Democrat* and landed a job at the much less affluent *St. Louis Republic* where his talents as a feature writer were appreciated, but the pay, $18 a week, remained low and he felt the time had come to try something else.

After a tearful farewell from Sara White, who from childhood had been known as "Jug," and doubtless promising undying fealty, Dreiser headed east, perhaps with New York in mind as his eventual destination. Newspapers in Cleveland and Buffalo had nothing to offer, but the city editor of the *Toledo Blade*, Arthur Henry, with whom he struck up an immediate friendship, thought that something might turn up within two or three weeks. When Dreiser reached Pittsburgh, a telegram from Henry was waiting for him, offering him a job. This proved helpful in getting himself hired by the *Pittsburgh Dispatch*. Pittsburgh, with its rivers and bridges, the contrast between the mansions of the steel barons and the wooden homes of the mill workers, the night sky lighted by the fiery steel plants, fascinated him for a time, but the deepest impression during his short stay came from the Carnegie Library. There he found a complete set of Balzac. Remembering the advice of the city editor of the *St. Louis Republic* that he read and emulate Balzac, he spent many mornings reading him in the library. It was in the same library that he first encountered Herbert Spencer and Thomas Huxley.

Spencer, as he was to write later, "nearly killed me." While Dreiser may not have given much heed to the strictures of Christianity concerning sexual relations, his Catholic upbringing had given him the comforting faith in a personal God, the belief that life had purpose and meaning, and it taught him to accept his own place in the order of being. Suddenly, as he said, his reading of Spencer "took every shred of belief away from me; showed me that I was a chemical atom in a whirl of unknown forces; the realization clouded my mind." In the despair and hopelessness that his reading of Spencer had left him, he decided to move on to New York—as his biographer, W. A. Swanberg describes his state of mind at the time, "Since one was hopeless anywhere, one might as well be hopeless in New York as in Pittsburgh." Late in November 1894 he gave up his job with the *Dispatch*. With $240 he had saved, he went on to New York, the irresistible magnet to the aspiring writer.

Of his work as a newspaperman in Pittsburgh, his biographer has this to say:

> While Dreiser had a remarkable capacity for getting facts twisted— a weakness he never conquered—the *Dispatch*, like his previous newspaper employers, found him effective at feature yarns wherein he could speculate, digress and dramatize. Dreiser wrote essays about Pittsburgh scenes and oddities with what he felt was the Balzac touch. He could find unusual sidelights in commonplace subjects, writing about cats, the Hancock Street morgue, hoboes, the mosquito menace, dog catchers, suicides and similar topics.

Dreiser soon discovered that however confident he may have been in his own destiny, New York was not waiting for him with open arms. After being rebuffed by one newspaper after another, he was finally able literally to force his way into the *New York World*, where he was to be paid at the rate of $7.50 per column for everything he wrote that went into the paper. On his first day he earned $1.86, and so it continued. He was inclined to be envious of his brother Paul's success and was therefore determined not to go to him for help, but after being reduced to living in a hotel for down-and-outers at 25¢ a night, he swallowed his pride and went to the music publishers, Howley, Haviland & Co., of which Paul was one of the principals, with an idea for a magazine which he would edit. Each issue was to include several popular songs, but its purpose was to promote the songs of Howley, Haviland. The publishers accepted the idea, and soon Theodore Dreiser was the editor of a magazine—*Ev'ry Month*—with a column, "Reflections," which often ran to several pages, in which he expressed his views on such subjects as foreign policy, social justice, the possibility of life on Mars, and, of course, the philosophy of Herbert Spencer. This column was signed "The Prophet." It is a tribute to the diligence and editorial skill of the editor that he was able to attract the readers and advertisers necessary to make the magazine profitable. But differences inevitably developed between the serious young editor and the publisher of such songs as *Moonlight Kisses Gavotte*, and after two years, in September 1897, *Ev'ry Month* appeared for the last time.

The years editing *Ev'ry Month* had given Dreiser invaluable experience and had opened doors for him to other magazines, which he lost no time taking advantage of. He worked hard developing ideas which he began to sell in such magazines as *Munsey's* and *Cosmopolitan*. He did a series of interviews of successful men—among others Marshall Field and P. D. Armour—for Orison Swett Marden, the founder of *Success* magazine, and wrote an article for *Ainslie's* on the use of carrier pigeons in wartime and one on a Connecticut cartridge factory for *Cosmopolitan* (this was during the war with Spain). In 1899 he was included in *Who's Who* as an editor, poet, author and contributor to such magazines as *The Saturday Evening Post* and *Cosmopolitan*. On December 28, 1898, after much prodding, he married the impatient "Jug," who had been waiting six years. The wedding took place not in her parents' Missouri home as she had hoped and planned, but privately in

Washington, an event he was later to describe ungallantly, as "the pale flame of duty."

In the summer following his marriage, Dreiser and his new wife joined his friend Arthur Henry and his wife for three happy months in a large, spacious house the Henrys had acquired on the Maumee River in Ohio. Henry greatly admired Dreiser's skill as a writer and was a welcome and stimulating companion. They both worked contentedly together, and when Dreiser and "Jug" went back to New York in September, Henry joined them with the intention of continuing their collaboration. Henry was writing a novel and, suggesting that they could work together, urged Dreiser to begin a novel also, or, at least, a short story. Dreiser did, with Henry's encouragement, write several short stories, and then one day, when Henry again suggested a novel, he picked up a piece of yellow paper, as he tells the story, and across the top wrote "Sister Carrie," perhaps unconsciously thinking of the career of his own sister Emma, who had eloped with a man from Chicago named Hopkins after he had looted the safe of his employer, Chapin & Gore, an elegant saloon. In an interview with Dorothy Dudley quoted in the Norton edition of *Sister Carrie*, she quotes Dreiser as answering, when she asked whether the name really came first and the characters and theme afterwards. "Yes, actually! My mind was blank except for the name. I had no idea who or what she was to be. I have often thought there was something mystic about it, as if I were being used, like a medium."

Whether there was anything mystic about it or not, it is a striking fact that one of the landmark novels of the twentieth century, a novel that marked a decisive change in literary style, should have been written in the last year of the nineteenth century by a young man of twenty-eight from a small town in Indiana.

The plot for *Sister Carrie* came ready-made from Dreiser's own family: his sister Emma became Carrie Meeber, Chapin & Gore became Fitzgerald & Moye, and L. A. Hopkins, the absconding manager of the elegant saloon, became George Hurstwood. What made the novel was not the story of a young, inexperienced girl from the country encountering the realities of the city, but what

Dreiser did with the story. Carrie left her first lover to elope with her second, and after becoming a successful actress, she abandoned him. She is not an inspiring character, and Hurstwood, who in his infatuation for Carrie deserts his family and finally destroys himself, is not even a slightly tragic figure, but for all that, *Sister Carrie* is a gripping novel. The characters who make up the story come alive, they are real people, and finally, they are presented with understanding and sympathy.

Carrie's first experience with the city is looking for a job, and no one would have known better than Dreiser what a disheartening experience that can be:

> With the wane of the afternoon went her hopes, her courage, and her strength. . . . She cast about vainly for some possible place to apply, but she found no door which she had the courage to enter. It would be the same thing all over. The old humiliation of her plea, rewarded by a curt denial. Sick at heart and in body, she turned to the west . . . and began that wearisome, baffled retreat which the seeker for employment at nightfall too often makes.

Then, becoming a successful and much sought-after actress, Carrie remarks to her friend Lola,

> "I get lonely, don't you?"
> "You oughtn't to get lonely," said Lola, thinking of Carrie's success. "There're lots would give their ears to be in your shoes."
> Carrie looked out again at the passing crowd.
> "I don't know," she said.
> Unconsciously her idle hands were beginning to weary.

When Hurstwood first appears he is a respected member of the community, affable, well-dressed, an active member of some Masonic organization, living in a comfortable house with his wife and two children. The last we hear of him: "A slow, black boat setting out from the pier at Twenty-seventh Street upon its weekly errand, bore with many others, his nameless body to Potter's Field." Dreiser is able to make the fate of this ordinary man so compelling, as inconsequential as it may have been in the tide of life, that the account of his step-by-step self-destruction is painful to read.

It was of such commonplace lives that Theodore Dreiser put together one of the classics of the twentieth century.

With Arthur Henry's encouragement, Dreiser worked through the fall and winter of 1899-1990 on *Sister Carrie*. At the same time, to earn money, he turned out magazine articles, one for *Harper's* for example, on fruit growing. He finished *Carrie* in the middle of April, the conclusion, after much difficulty, finally coming to him in a burst of inspiration while lying in the sun in Palisades Park:

> Oh, Carrie, Carrie! Oh, blind strivings of the human heart! . . .
> Know, then, that for you is neither surfeit nor content. In your
> rocking-chair, by your window, dreaming, shall you long, alone. In
> your rocking-chair, by your window, shall you dream such happi-
> ness as you may never feel.

The initial response of publishers, critics, and the reading public to *Sister Carrie* is of the greatest interest and a significant chapter in literary history. Dreiser first offered the manuscript to Harpers, where he was known and respected as a contributor to their magazines. After their rather prompt rejection—"a superior piece of reportorial realism, but it will not sell"—early in 1900 he took it to Doubleday, Page & Co. where Frank Norris, the author of *McTeague*, a successful recent novel which Dreiser admired, was a reader-editor. Norris, the first in the firm to read the manuscript, recommended it highly for publication. His recommendation makes it apparent that *Sister Carrie* had given him the exhilarating experience every editor hopes for but rarely encounters, that of discovering a great book. In a letter to Dreiser he speaks of his recommendation to members of the firm:

> I said, and it gives me pleasure to repeat it, that it was the best
> novel I had read in MS. since I had been reading for the firm, and it
> pleases me as well as any novel I have read in *any* form, published
> or otherwise.

This was followed by a letter on June 9 from Walter Hines Page, in Frank Doubleday's absence in Europe the acting head of the firm, congratulating the author on "so good a piece of work," which was soon followed by an agreement to publish the manuscript. Dreiser was overjoyed, and believing that *Sister Carrie* was now safely on the way to publication went with his new wife for a visit to her parents' farm in Missouri.

When Mr. Doubleday returned from Europe and had a chance to read the proofs, the firm began to have second thoughts about whether they wanted such a book on their list. Mr. Doubleday objected on the grounds that it was immoral and would not sell. Mrs. Doubleday seems to have strongly agreed with her husband. Dreiser, in recounting the story of the suppression of his first novel, made much of Mrs. Doubleday's part in this episode, but how much influence she really had in the final decision seems doubtful. It is probable that the decision to ask Dreiser to release Doubleday from the contract was based as much or more on business consideration as on the alleged immorality of the book. In any case, when Page asked Dreiser to release them from the contract, Dreiser, with the encouragement of Arthur Henry, refused. After the exchange of numerous letters and Page's offer to help Dreiser find another publisher, Dreiser demanded that the contract be fulfilled, to which Doubleday snapped, "All right. You stand on your legal rights and we'll stand on ours." The book was published November 9, 1900 by a reluctant publisher in an edition of 1,000 copies, and except for the 127 review copies Frank Norris sent out, in many cases with a letter of recommendation, it got no support whatever from the publisher. Doubleday was careful, it should be said, on the advice of their attorney, to fill orders promptly. It was widely reviewed and while most reviewers condemned the book for "immorality" and its alleged "philosophy of despair," some critics did recognize the strength of the book and a few "even saw greatness" in the author, according to Dreiser's biographer's account.

Neither the critics nor the public in 1900, it seems clear, were prepared to accept the realistic picture of American life Dreiser presented to them. During the first year after publication, 456 copies were sold, yielding Dreiser a royalty of $68.40. Americans in the early 1900s obviously preferred romance to realism— *Graustark*, for example, sold 300,000 copies while *Sister Carrie* sold less than five hundred, and *Mrs. Wiggs of the Cabbage Patch* sold 170,000. *Graustark*, however, except as a literary curiosity is long since forgotten, while *Sister Carrie* occupies a firm place among the classics of American literature, as is demonstrated by the Norton paperback edition, which includes, besides 373 pages of well-printed text, 216 pages of "Background and Sources" together with essays by such distinguished critics as Kenneth S. Lynn, Charles C. Walcutt, David Pizer and William L. Phillips.

The reviewers of the somewhat shortened English edition, being able to view the book from a distance, correctly considered it not as social criticism, but as literature. The *Manchester Guardian*, for example, was of the opinion that *Carrie* "should belong to the veritable documents of American history," and the *London Daily Chronicle* called Dreiser "a true artist." Amusingly enough, Heineman, the English publisher, wrote to Doubleday to say that he considered *Carrie* "the best book we have recently published, and are likely to publish for many a long day," and congratulated him for having discovered such an author. All this may have been encouraging to Dreiser, but with the one hundred dollars the English edition brought him and the royalties from Doubleday, he had less than two hundred dollars to show for the four months of intensive work he had put into *Carrie*, and this at a time when he would otherwise have been earning more than a hundred dollars a week writing for magazines.

Dreiser's life up to this time had been in preparation for *Carrie*. His boyhood in small towns in Indiana, the struggles of his mother in the face of poverty and misfortune to keep her family together, his own fight as a boy of sixteen to make his way in Chicago, his experience as a newspaperman, all went into *Carrie*. When the timid, inexperienced Carrie fresh from a small town faces the frightening prospect of seeking work in Chicago, which she desperately needs, Dreiser, in describing her plight, is clearly suffering with her, as he did with Hurstwood when he describes him, cold and hungry, being pushed from the stage door into the snow after a futile attempt to see Carrie. Dreiser was above all else a writer; when he wrote *Carrie* he put everything he had into it and he was well aware that he had produced a major book, all of which made its initial failure the more devastating.

The failure of *Carrie* was followed by a severe, debilitating depression. Dreiser had started a second novel, *Jennie Gerhardt*, for which he had a contract and an advance, to be paid monthly, but after the first few chapters was unable to continue. Efforts to write magazine articles led only to rejections. He stayed for a time in small towns in Virginia and Delaware, walked for many miles, hoping that this would restore his equanimity, but all in vain. Coming back to New York with $32 in his pocket he stayed for a time in a miserable room in Brooklyn that cost $1.25 a week. On the verge of suicide, he ran into his brother Paul, who was shocked by his appearance, gave him the $75 he had in his pocket, and arranged for him to go to a "repair shop" for overindulged millionaires operated on Long Island by Paul's friend, William Muldoon, a former wrestling champion. This was followed by working for several weeks in a shop of the New York Central Railroad. By Christmas, 1903, he was able to write: "After a long battle I am once more the possessor of health. . . . I have fought a battle for the right to live and for the present, musing with stilled nerves and a serene gaze, I seem the victor."

Dreiser began his literary comeback by working for magazines, becoming editor, after several lesser jobs, of *Smith's Magazine*, whose circulation he pushed to 125,000. From there he went on to *Broadway*, which he made into a frothy magazine designed to appeal to an audience that appreciated such departments as "Beautiful Women of New York" or "Summer Hostesses of Society." By now he had enough money to buy the plates for *Carrie*, which he was determined to see properly published. A Chicago critic, Edna Kenton, had helped to revive critical interest in the book by distributing remaindered copies to her friends, and his assistant at *Broadway*, to whom he confided his frustration at the failure of *Carrie*, discussed the problem with her friend Flora Mai Holly, one of the first literary agents in New York. Miss Holly arranged with the new firm, B. W. Dodge & Co., to bring out a new edition of *Carrie*. Dreiser, who seems to have had the usual writer's distrust of publishers, invested $5,000 in the new firm to keep himself informed of what was going on and became secretary and editor. He also lent the plates for the new edition and threw himself into the preparations for its promotion. On May 18, 1907, the new edition of *Sister Carrie* appeared with recommendations from such literary figures as Brand Whitlock, Hamlin Garland and Albert Bigelow Paine. In advertising the book, great care was taken, his biographer points out ... "in an effort to attract lowbrows interested in sex without offending highbrows demanding literature." The new edition was more widely reviewed than the first and generally far more favorably. The *New York World* praised its "uncommon quality," the *San Francisco Call* described it as "a work of genius," and while not a bestseller, by September *Carrie* had sold 4,617 copies.

Dreiser felt vindicated, all the more so when he was offered the editorship of the *Delineator*, the most successful women's magazine of the time with a circulation close to one million. It would seem to have been particularly incongruous that Dreiser, of all people, should have been made editor of a magazine that prided itself on being the country's largest distributor of dress patterns and the bastion, so to speak, of domestic bliss and stability. In the new editor's first issue he announced, "A BIGGER DELINEATOR ... *The Delineator's* message is human betterment. Its appeal is to the one great humanizing force of humanity—womanhood." But as cynical as this may have sounded from a man who spoke of his marriage "as a torture" and "as a binding state and I was not to be bound," Dreiser was a highly skilled editor. He had a keen sense for what would appeal to his readers, as a writer himself was an unerring judge of the writing of others, and quickly put a qualified staff together which he ruled with an iron hand. His biographer offers the following account of an editorial conference under Dreiser:

> Nervous, moody, he kept popping his ribboned pince nez off and on, fiddling with his handkerchief. He was tough, sarcastic, even cruel, driving his staff and himself, demanding ideas that would sell more magazines and thus more patterns, holding weekly editorial conferences that sometimes lasted into evening, usually quiet and considerate but sometimes wounding in his sarcasm. He was consciously advancing his destiny in accordance with his conviction that life was a struggle in which one either was a leader who drove others or was one of the driven.

With his big, luxurious office and large staff, as the successful and respected editor of a leading magazine, after the despair of a few months before, Dreiser, as his biographer puts it, "was as happy as a misanthrope could be." There were setbacks, of course: in spite of Dreiser's efforts to be helpful, his new publisher, B. W. Dodge, failed, and a new magazine he had started as a sideline, the *Bohemian*, was discontinued only after a few months, but he seemed finally to be firmly on his feet. It was during this time with the *Delineator* that his friendship began with H. L. Mencken, which, with the ups and downs to be expected in the association of two such self-willed men, lasted for many years and contributed substantially to Dreiser's literary career. In the summer of 1909, he asked Mencken, whose writing he admired, to ghostwrite articles on the care and feeding of babies for a Baltimore pediatrician. Mencken, nine years younger than Dreiser, appeared in his office, his hair plastered down and parted in the middle, wearing yellow shoes and a loud tie, self-confident to the point of cockiness. Dreiser, much amused, greeted Mencken, "Well, well, if it isn't Anheuser's brightest boy out to see the town." Mencken, not to be outdone, replied that he was indeed the son of the richest brewer in town, but in his case Baltimore rather than St. Louis.

With a man of Dreiser's temperament, not to say roving eye, working as top man in an office full of women, complications were inevitable. It all began with an assistant editor, Anne Ericsson Cudlipp, an attractive widow from Richmond, who soon established a bond of friendship with Dreiser's wife. In the course of this association, Dreiser met Mrs. Cudlipp's seventeen-year-old daughter, Thelma, and became infatuated. Dreiser, tall and awkward as he was, took up dancing to further his courtship, and after her mother sent the girl to South Carolina to isolate her with relatives, began to write long, passionate letters, addressing her as "Honeypot"—"Jug's" name for him was "Honeybugs." At Mrs. Cudlipp's strict instructions, the letters never reached their destination. The situation was made all the more ludicrous by Dreiser's directions on the envelopes, "Personal delivery only—return receipt demanded." In desperation, Mrs. Cudlipp finally informed Dreiser that unless he desisted in his attention to her daughter she would inform management and demand his dismissal, and this was no idle threat; as of October 1, 1910 Dreiser was dismissed as editor of the

Delineator, with the public announcement that he had been given a year's leave of absence. Painful as this undignified affair had been for him, it had the fortunate result of bringing him back to his literary career. The first consequence was the completion of *Jennie Gerhardt*, which may well be the book that above all others demonstrates the qualities that made Dreiser more than an ordinary writer—sympathy, understanding, and most of all pity for the human condition, but, it must also be said, his sympathy was for man in the abstract, for the characters in his novels rather than for men and women of flesh and blood.

The plot of *Jennie Gerhardt* is as simple and straightforward as that of *Sister Carrie* and doubtless drew as heavily on the experiences of Dreiser's own family. The book begins at the front desk of the leading hotel in Columbus, Ohio, in the fall of 1880. A middle-aged woman is asking the clerk if there might be any work in the hotel for her daughter, who is standing in the background, timid and shamefaced at being the subject of such attention. Dreiser's description of the mother with its pity and understanding for her situation sets the tone of the whole book. The mother, he said,

> ... was a helpless, fleshy build, with a frank, open countenance and an innocent, diffident manner. Her eyes were large and patient, and in them dwelt such a shadow of distress as only those who have looked sympathetically into the countenances of the distraught and helpless poor know anything about.

The girl who, of course, is the subject of the novel, is the oldest of six children of a family that is having a hard time. The father, a glass-blower by trade, has been ill and out of work. Mrs. Gerhardt, we are told, is "no weakling." Besides dressing the children, cooking, mending, taking care of her sick husband, she takes in washing when she can get it, and now, in desperation, has gone to the hotel to find work for her daughter Jennie. On the way home, she is able to get bread and bacon, on credit, for supper.

It is arranged that Jennie will work in the hotel three afternoons a week, but will also do any laundry for the hotel's most distinguished guest, Senator Brander. The senator, who is unmarried, is much taken by Jennie's comely, open face and ingratiating manner, becomes interested in her, and comes to visit the family, much to the annoyance of the father, who is German and a strict, devout Lutheran. The senator is helpful to the family, and when Jennie's brother is arrested for throwing down coal from a railroad car, to be picked up by one of his brothers, Jennie goes to the senator for help. The stress of the situation and the emotional response of the senator's growing attachment is too much for her, and Jennie discovers in a few weeks that she is pregnant. The senator promises to marry her, as he doubtless intended to do, but having lost an election, must go first to Washington to wind up his affairs. While there he dies from a heart attack.

Jennie's father is outraged by what he considers a disgrace to his family and puts his daughter out of the house. When it comes time to baptize the child, however, he relents and with his wife acts as sponsor. It says much about Dreiser that as contemptuous as he undertook to be of religion, he recognizes the beautiful Lutheran rite of baptism, and describes Gerhardt's response to it with reverence and sincerity:

> As this solemn admonition was read a feeling of obligation descended upon the grandfather of this little outcast; a feeling that he was bound to give this tiny creature lying on his wife's arm the care and attention which God in His sacrament has commanded. He bowed his head in utmost reverence, and when the service was concluded and they left the silent church he was without words to express his feelings. Religion was a consuming thing with him. God was a person, a dominant reality. Religious was not a thing of mere words or interesting ideas to be listened to on Sunday, but a strong, vital expression of the Divine Will handed down from a time when men were in personal contact with God. Its fulfillment was a matter of joy and salvation with him, the one consolation of a creature sent to wander in a vale whose explanation was not here but in heaven.

How is one to reconcile the man who could write so beautifully of the faith of old Gerhardt with the man who invariably spoke of religion with contempt and could write, "In short, I catch no meaning from all I have seen, and pass quite as I came, confused and dismayed." But it was not the same man. The Dreiser who wrote of old Gerhardt's religion as a "vital expression of the Divine Will" was the artist, a man possessed by the gift of creativity, while the forty-year-old man who addressed letters to a seventeen-year-old girl as "Honeypot" was Dreiser the lascivious man. When he described old Gerhardt's religious faith—and the character of Gerhardt was clearly inspired by Dreiser's own father—he was expressing something that came from the innermost recesses of his being, which he himself may not have been conscious of. Even H. L. Mencken, for whom skepticism was almost an article of faith, could speak of the power of the image evoked by Dreiser as ". . . not only brilliant on the surface, but mysterious and appealing in its depth."

Wyndham Lewis, who, as painter and writer, had direct experience of the act of creativity, made some striking observations on the subject in his book, *Time and Western Man*. "I will state very briefly my own belief as to the true character of artistic creation. The production of a work of art is, I believe, strictly the work of a visionary. Indeed, this seems so evident that it scarcely needs pointing out. . . . If you say that creative art is a spell, a talisman, an incarnation—that it is *magic*, in short, there, too, I believe you would be correctly describing it. That the artist uses and manipulates a supernatural power seems very likely."

But to get back to Dreiser's story. In their search for work, the Gerhardt family moves to Cleveland where Jennie is able to establish herself as a lady's maid in a prominent family. The unassuming, winning manner and youthful beauty that had appealed to Senator Brander soon caught the eye of a friend who was visiting the family, Lester Kane, rich, unmarried, in his thirties, a vigorous, handsome man. In describing the impression Jennie made on him to the woman he eventually married, Kane tells her, "Well, anyhow, I lost my head. I thought she was the most perfect thing under the sun, even if she was a little out of my world. . . . I thought that I could just take her, and then—well, you know. That is where I made my mistake. I didn't think that would prove as serious as it did."

Overwhelmed by the attention of the worldly, self-confident Lester Kane and his promise of assistance to her struggling mother,

Jennie succumbs and agrees to live with him. He tells her that he loves her and believes that he does, but not enough to face the disapproval of his family and the social opprobrium that marriage to a servant girl would bring. Kane's business interests—his family are successful manufacturers of wagons and carriages—bring him to Chicago where he eventually buys a large house in a fashionable neighborhood. They live quietly, their unmarried state excluding them from the social life that would otherwise have been appropriate to Kane's wealth and position. Vesta, the child of Jennie's relationship with Senator Brander, joins them, and after the death of her mother, her father is brought into the household. Jennie is by nature what, before the days of feminism, was approvingly called a homemaker, and does everything in her power to make Kane comfortable and contented, but suffers from her exclusion from marriage and a normal family, which she accepts, however, as the consequence of what she calls her "badness."

H. L. Mencken in the review which appeared with its first publication in 1911 pronounced *Jennie Gerhardt* one of the great American novels. One does not need to accept everything Mencken says about it to agree with his conclusion—it is a great novel. The skill and consistency with which Dreiser develops and contrasts the two central characters give the novel its substance and quality. Jennie going alone from Lester's funeral to the railroad station, hoping desperately to have a chance at least to see Lester's coffin as it is loaded on the train, is exactly the sort of person we might have expected when we first met her at the age of eighteen. But life hasn't been kind to her. After fathering her child and promising to marry her, Senator Brander unexpectedly dies; Lester Kane, who always treated her generously, with Jennie's encouragement, marries the woman his family approves of, thus saving his inheritance; and finally her own promising daughter, to whom she is passionately devoted and who is all she has, dies in a typhoid epidemic; but for all that, in trying to discern for herself some order and purpose in the seeming contradictions of life, she is able to say to herself, "Did anything matter except goodness—goodness of heart? What else was there that was real?"

Lester Kane, by way of contrast, is described as "an essentially animal man, pleasantly veneered by education and background." Like many other Americans whose Irish grandfathers dug canals, built railroads, carried bricks and mortar in a new country, he "was strong, hairy, axiomatic, and witty." He was born a Catholic, "but no longer a believer in the divine inspiration of Catholicism." He has none of the unswerving, uncompromising faith of Jennie's father. Lester Kane, we are led to believe, is a pleasant, attractive man, successful in business, but lacks the drive that made it possible for his father to build a large manufacturing enterprise. He accepts what life offers without any strong feeling of obligation to give anything in return. In many ways, he is a rather typical son, or grandson, of a successful, self-made man.

Jennie, however inferior her social status may be, is a far superior person. Lester may think that he loves Jennie, he treats her kindly, takes her to Europe, but he is unwilling to risk the disfavor of his family and especially the loss of his inheritance to marry her. Jennie, on the other hand, when his old flame reappears, the rich, beautiful Letty Pace, urges him to marry her, great as the blow to her would be, because she thinks it would make a more satisfying life for him. Her love for him includes the willingness to make such a sacrifice for his happiness. When Lester is dying, however, it is Jennie that he asks for.

As similar as these first two novels of Theodore Dreiser are, particularly in their dependence on the experiences of members of his own family, *Jennie Gerhardt*, in writing and structure is the better book, but more than that, Jennie herself is a far superior character to Carrie. It is Jennie, with the strength of character to meet the demands of life without sacrificing her self-respect or personal integrity, who makes her story a great novel.

The critical response to *Jennie Gerhardt*, while not entirely favorable, was far warmer than that accorded to *Sister Carrie*. H. L. Mencken, who became almost a sales agent for the book, was not alone in his praise. Franklin P. Adams, in a letter to Dreiser, told him, "*Jennie Gerhardt* is a great book and I salute and congratulate you earnestly and reverently." Floyd Dell, in the *Chicago Post*, a much respected and influential newspaper in those days, in a full-page review agreed: "I may say, without saying it in vain, this is a great book." There were, of course, other options. The Lexington, Kentucky, *Herald* called the book "utterly base," and the *Chicago Herald* compared its style to that of a "proficient stenographer." While not a bestseller, by the end of the first year, it had sold 7,700 copies. After the disaster of *Carrie*, this was quite respectable, but not enough to satisfy the author, who began looking for a different publisher and the advances which would enable him to go to Europe to gather material on Charles Yerkes, on whose career he planned to base his next book.

Having devoted his first pair of novels to the fate of two young women from modest, not to say impoverished, circumstances making their way in the world seemingly dominated by men, and men, moreover, who appeared ready to take advantage of them at every opportunity, Dreiser now turned to a quite different subject, the ruthless, ambitious male, this in the form of Charles T. Yerkes, the traction magnate, to whom he gave the name Frank Cowperwood. He wrote three Cowperwood novels: *The Financier* (1912), *The Titan* (1914), and *The Stoic* (1947). What was it about Charles Yerkes, it seems fair to ask, to have justified the immense amount of work Dreiser put into gathering the story of his life and weaving it into three long, detailed novels? It seems probable that it was Yerkes' daring that fascinated Dreiser, his readiness to defy convention and the accepted rules of conduct, not only in business, but also in his relations with women: he was always seeking, but never finding, the "perfect woman." Furthermore, in spite of his defiance of the rules, a defiance which involved the wholesale bribing of legislatures, and aldermen, Yerkes made a success of his professional life, leaving Chicago an efficient street railway system and, in the process, making a large fortune for himself.

The Financier, the first book of the trilogy, is an account of Cowperwood's career in his native Philadelphia as a spectacularly successful financial manipulator, which ended with a term in the federal penitentiary. Following his release from prison and the recovery of his fortune in the wake of the panic brought on by the failure of Jay Cooke & Co., he decided that Chicago, rebuilding itself after the Great Fire, offered a unique opportunity for a man of his talent and ambition to make a fresh start. The first chapter of

The Titan, the second book in the trilogy, is a striking example of Dreiser's phenomenal talent for story-telling. In less than five pages he sets the stage and invites, one can say almost compels, the participation of the reader in his account of the career of a successful, strong-willed, and, in many ways, reprehensible but fascinating man.

The Titan begins in a Philadelphia railroad station, with Cowperwood bidding farewell to the beautiful Aileen Butler as he prepares to take the train to Chicago. "We'll fix on some place," he tells her, "and then you watch me settle this fortune question. We'll not live under a cloud always. I'll get a divorce, and we'll marry and things will come out right with a bang. Money will do that." Arriving in Chicago the second morning out, he is not at all turned off by the flat countryside, the drab wooden houses, and the irregular wooden sidewalks. Rather he is impressed by the grain elevators, the busy railroad yards, the lumber schooners in the river, the evidence of bustling activity. For him, "This raw, dirty town seemed naturally to compose itself into a stirring artistic picture. Why, it fairly sang! The world was young here. Life was doing something new." On the way to the Grand Pacific Hotel, which he had chosen as "the one with the most social significance," he studied the streets, particularly noticing "the little yellow, blue, green, white and brown streetcars" and the bony horses that pulled them. "They were flimsy affairs, these cars, merely highly varnished kindling-wood with bits of polished brass and glass stuck about them, but he realized what fortunes they portended if the city grew. Streetcars, he knew, were his natural vocation. Even more than stock brokerage, even more than banking, even more than stock organization, he loved the thought of streetcars and the vast manipulative life it suggested."

The period of Chicago history covered by *The Titan*, roughly the last two decades of the nineteenth century, was a time of phenomenal growth. From a population of 500,000 in 1880, Chicago by 1900 had reached 1,700,000 with all that this could mean, among other things, as Cowperwood had observed upon his arrival, to those who controlled public transportation. "Chicago was a good place to make money"—a realization that has brought many others besides Charles Yerkes to Chicago.

It will be remembered that Dreiser arrived in Chicago as a boy of sixteen in 1887. After various menial jobs, he became a newspaper reporter, leaving the city in 1892 for a St. Louis newspaper. He had had the opportunity, therefore, to learn to know Chicago "in the raw," so to speak, and with his remarkable ability to observe, to gather and organize facts into a story, was uniquely equipped to describe Chicago through the career of the towering figure of Charles Yerkes. Such a book as *The Titan*, of course, is not history in the usual sense—there are no footnotes, the names of the characters have been changed, although in many cases still recognizable, and the facts have doubtless been altered to fit the flow of the narrative. But for all that Dreiser has given us a picture of how the upper level of Chicago, whether in business, politics or what was known as "society," conducted itself during those years of frantic growth. While perhaps not accurate in detail, in broad outline it is true. Furthermore, the Chicago described in *The Titan*, let us face it, is in more ways than we of Chicago might care to admit, the Chicago of today.

The book that followed *The Titan* by only a year, *Hoosier Holiday*, gives the impression of having been written as a welcome change of pace. The writing of *Carrie* and *Jennie*, involved as they were with the lives of members of his own family, must have required a substantial emotional commitment on Dreiser's part, and the account of the hurt caused to his wife by Cowperwood's marital transgressions could only have been written with the awareness of similar transgressions on his own part and what they must have meant to his own wife. *Hoosier Holiday* has no such problems; it is an account of what is described as a thoroughly enjoyable automobile trip in 1915, before the days of superhighways, of motels, monster trucks, traffic congestion and all the rest, from New York to the various towns in Indiana where Dreiser had lived with his family before leaving for Chicago at the age of sixteen. His companion on the trip, Franklin Booth, who supplied the car and chauffeur with the understanding that they would share the cost of replacing "blow-outs," also came from Indiana, having made a successful career in New York as an artist. His drawings of towns, houses, and landscapes made as they drove along add greatly to the charm of the book.

Hoosier Holiday is a nostalgic book, nostalgic for Dreiser for its memories of his mother, of his brothers and sisters, of the fragrance of the woods and fields of the Indiana countryside of his boyhood. For the reader it is a nostalgic book also, a look back to the America of small towns and country roads, as the country was before it was crisscrossed by great highways and overwhelmed by cars and trucks. There are many beautiful descriptions in *Hoosier Holiday*. The following is from a recollection of fishing with his brother Ed in the Busseron, a small river near the town of Sullivan:

And then late in the afternoon, after hours of this wonder world, we trudge home, along the warm, dusty, yellow country road; the evening sun is red in the West, our feet buried in the dust. Not a wagon, not a sound, save that of wood doves, bluejays, the spiri-tual, soulful, lyric thrush. On a long, limp twig with a fork at the end is strung *our* fish, so small and still now— so large, glistening, brilliant when we caught them. On every hand are field fragrances, the distant low of cows and the grunts of pigs. I hear the voice of a farmer—"Poo-gy! Poogy! Poogy!"

"Gee, ma kin fry these—huh?"

"You bet."

Brown-legged, dusty, tired, we tramp back to the kitchen door. There she is, plump, tolerant, smiling—a gentle, loving under-standing of boys and their hungry, restless ways written all over her face.

"Yes, they're fine. We'll have them for supper. Wash and clean them, and then wash your hands and feet and come in."

H. L. Menken, who knew and appreciated Dreiser as few others, has this to say about *Hoosier Holiday* in his *A Book of Prefaces*:

I know, indeed, of no book which better describes the American hinterland. Here we have no idle spying by a stranger, but a full-length representation by one who knows the things he describes in-timately, and is himself a part of it. Almost every mile of the road traveled has been Dreiser's own road in life. . . . And so he does his chronicle *con amore*, with many a sentimental dredging up of old memories, old hopes and old dreams.

As warm and appealing as such descriptions are, *Hoosier Holiday* is not all nostalgia. Encountering an attractive, young girl in an Indiana town, Dreiser's thoughts, not surprisingly, turn to the relationship between man and woman, which leads to the subject of monogamy. "We hear much of one life, one love," he begins, "but how many actually attain to that ideal—if it is one." The subject of monogamy, one senses, seems to put him unconsciously on the defensive. "Personally I have found it not only possible, but by a curious and entirely fortuitous combination of circumstances almost affectionately unavoidable, to hold three, four—even as many as five and six—women in regard or the emotional compass of myself, at one and the same time, not all to the same degree, perhaps, or in the same way, but each for certain qualities which the others do not possess."

These extramarital relationships may have been artistically stimulating and personally satisfying to Dreiser, but they were not appreciated by either of his two wives, nor, apparently by all of "those strange, affectionately dependent artistic souls he speaks of," as his biographer describes them. On the other hand, he reports, Thelma Cudlipp, many years after Dreiser's unrequited infatuation, had warm memories of him: "Of course Theo was anything but handsome, but there was a kind of grandeur about him." His biographer also quotes Ann Watkins, his assistant when he was editor of *Everybody's* magazine, as remarking "He was a tremendously physical person, without conventional morals, almost ugly, and yet he had a kindliness and warmth that were magnetic." And his two wives, for all his transgressions, were devoted to him.

After all this, what is one to say about Theodore Dreiser? We can first agree that he was a serious, dedicated writer. Writing was his life. It is true that when he needed money he could turn out the sort of things the popular magazines wanted—interviews with millionaires describing the secret of their success, an account of a cartridge factory in wartime, but in his first book, *Sister Carrie*, he is utterly uncompromising—he shows American life as he had experienced it, adamantly refusing to conform to the demands of his publisher, to the opinions of the critics, or to anyone else. He knew where he stood and what he wanted to say, and in his best work, he did so.

In *An American Tragedy*, based closely on a sensational murder and trial that fascinated him, Dreiser finally managed the rare feat of writing a book that was recognized as a literary classic and a bestseller. He was not a great stylist, but his books had a compelling quality that is inescapable. Cowperwood, the character based on Charles Yerkes in *The Titan*, is a strong personality, and while not in any way an admirable character, captures and holds the attention of the reader. When the leading financial men of Chicago believe that they are in a position to destroy him, by driving him into a corner and cutting off his credit, they summon him to an evening meeting in the house of a prominent banker. Cowperwood has prepared himself for just such an eventuality and is the complete master of the situation, as Dreiser is also in his account of it. Cowperwood, for all his faults, his selfishness, his overpowering ambition, his ruthlessness, is completely consistent and convincing, as is Jennie Gerhardt in her very different way. In her loyalty to Lester Kane she is true to herself, and when Dreiser has her say, after all the sorrows life has meted out to her, "Did anything matter except goodness—goodness of heart? What else was there that was real?" he wanted us to believe that life had not overwhelmed her.

In the uncompromising way he faces reality and equally so in the way in which he drives a situation to its ultimate conclusion, Dreiser reveals qualities, or failings, depending on one's point of view, which are characteristically German. When Hurstwood in *Sister Carrie* takes the first step on the downward path by taking Carrie for a drive on Washington Boulevard, the road of self-destruction doesn't end until his body is taken to Potter's Field in New York. There is no half-way for Dreiser. As a German would put it, *wenn schon, denn schon*.

In being able to create such a character as Jennie Gerhardt, Dreiser tells us, it seems clear, that what she represents was much more a part of his real person than all his talk about chemism, of being nothing more than a "chemical atom in a whirl of unknown forces," and in being able to create such a book as *Jennie Gerhardt*, Dreiser, with all his faults, it also seems clear, shows us that he was a great writer.

PART FOUR

Raising the Vision of
His Contemporaries

Louis Sullivan

Louis H. Sullivan:
Visionary and Architect*

Upbringing and Education

ON THE MONOLITH erected by architects and builders in Chicago's Graceland Cemetery to honor Louis Sullivan, there is the following inscription:

> By his buildings great in influence and power; his drawings unsurpassed in originality and beauty; his writings rich in poetry and prophecy; his teachings persuasive and eloquent; his philosophy where, in "Form Follows Function," he summed up all the truth in Art, Sullivan has earned his place as one of the greatest architectural forces in America.

This is only one of the lasting monuments to Sullivan's memory. His own work aside, Chicago's downtown cluster of skyscrapers, rising abruptly from the prairie landscape, overlooking the lake, is startling and spectacular, a tribute to his inspiration. Finally, there is his book, *The Autobiography of an Idea*† which remains to be read today, still fresh with his insights, graced with his genius.

He began writing his autobiography in 1922 and he finished it in 1924, a few months before his death at the age of sixty-eight. When he wrote his book he was living in a single room in a rather run-down Chicago hotel, dependent for his needs on the generosity of friends. He had long since given up his architect's office with its spectacular view of Lake Michigan in the tower of one of his greatest buildings, the Chicago Auditorium, the tower, as he

---

* Reprinted, with some changes, from *Modern Age*, Summer 1991.

† *The Autobiography of an Idea* was published serially in *Journal of the American Institute of Architects*, June 1922-August 1923. Published in book form by the A.I.A. press, 1924; reprinted by W. W. Norton & Co. in their "White Oak Library Series," 1934.

remarks in his book, that "holds its head in the air." It was in this office that Frank Lloyd Wright had worked as one of his draftsmen. Having been one of the great architects of his time and having designed many of its landmark buildings, by the time he wrote his book, he was reduced to preparing plans for the front of a modest music store, his last commission. For all the grimness of his circumstances, there is no trace of self-pity or bitterness in his book; on the contrary, reading it gives the distinct impression of the pleasure and satisfaction it must have given him to relive his life and to bring back the memories that writing it required.

In its intensity and passion, Sullivan's story of his life is a unique contribution to the cultural achievement of his time, but the sense it conveys of having lived his life to the full, of having taken advantage of its opportunities and met its challenges, gives the book its classic quality.

The Autobiography of an Idea is written in the third person. As the title indicates, it is not so much the story of Sullivan's life as an account of his development as an architect and of his conception of the task of the architect. In his book, Sullivan, who always refers to himself as Louis, views himself from a distance. He tells us what we need to know about his family background, of the circumstances of his growing up, of the influence of his parents, and especially of his grandparents, who played an important role in his life, of his teachers, of his training as an architect, but he tells us almost nothing about his personal life. His marriage is not so much as mentioned. Nor is there any mention of his brother, with whom he had a very close relationship until his brother's marriage, or of friendships, or of associations with other people except insofar as they were related to his development and career as an architect. The title of his book, it seems apparent, was carefully chosen and describes exactly what it is.

His father, Patrick Sullivan, was born in Ireland and from the age of twelve was entirely on his own, having become separated at a county fair from his father, whom he never saw again. The young man supported himself as a country fiddler, became a dancing teacher, and later conducted a successful dancing school in London. In 1847, Patrick Sullivan sailed for Boston, where he set up an academy and was successful. He was always successful, his son remarks; "His probity was such that he could always command desirable influence and respect." In Boston Patrick Sullivan met and married Andriene F. List. She was born in Geneva, Switzerland, was well brought up, a good pianist and a great asset to her husband's academy, the possibility of which, Sullivan says, his father perceived when he first met her. Sullivan speaks of his father as "merely self-centered—not even cold. He was moderate of habit; drank a little wine, smoked an occasional cigar, and was an enthusiast regarding hygiene." He respected his father, who taught him to swim at an early age, trained him to develop himself physically, and gave him the benefit of what he had learned of life from his own harsh encounter with reality in growing up, but it was his mother and grand-mother whom he loved with all the devotion of which he was capable. His mother's mother was French, her father, Henry W. List, a well-educated skeptical German from Hannover. Much of Louis' childhood was spent with his mother's parents on a "miniature farm," as he describes it, near a small town, Wakefield, north of Boston. Those early years were a happy, carefree time for him and played an important part in his development as a strong-willed man and creative architect. His grandfather recognized and encouraged Louis' interest in nature, his curiosity, and his desire to understand the world about him. His mother and grandmother encouraged and stimulated his talent for drawing and also his awareness and appreciation of beauty.

The various religious views of his parents and grandparents were quite different. None of these views was what might be called orthodox, except for those of his grandmother, but there was no conflict on such matters, and they seemed to have reconciled them in a way to have given Louis a healthy and responsible view of life. His mother's ideal, he writes in his book,

> . . . was a righteous man, sound of head and clean of heart, a truthful man, too natural to lie or to evade. These outbursts of his mother sank deep into the being of her son; and in looking back adown the years, he has reason justly to appraise in reverence and love a nature so transparent, so pure, so vehement, so sound, so filled with a yearning for the joy of life, so innocent, ecstatic in contemplation of beauty. . . .

His French grandmother, as he put it,

> ... alone was devout. Quietly she believed in her God; in the com-
> passion of His Son, in the wondrous love He bore. . . . She was
> satisfied to abide in her faith, undisturbed and undisturbing. Per-
> haps this is why her grandson loved her so. Innocent of creed, of
> doctrine and dogma, he loved her because she was good, he loved
> her because she was true, he loved her because to his adoring eyes
> she was beautiful.

On the other hand, his Grandfather List, who is said to have been
educated for the priesthood, "looked upon religion as a curious and
amusing human weakness—as conclusive evidence of universal stu-
pidity." As much as his grandfather ridiculed many things, including religious faith, "He never poked fun at the solar system. In this
domain, and the star-laden firmament, he lived his real life. This was
his grand passion. All else was trivial. The vastness awed him; the
brilliance inspired him."

Our author had been given the name Louis, but had never been
baptized, a problem, as he says, which "called for a family council."
His account of this event, which must have become a part of the
family lore, describes in a noncommittal and detached way the
various religious influences in the family and the manner of recon-
ciling them:

> The father, a nominal Free-mason, was not sure whether he was a
> Catholic or an Orangeman, or anything in particular, expressed no
> serious interest; he would leave it to the rest. Grandpa, as usual,
> vented his view in scornful laughter. Grandma, a Mennonite, was
> opposed to baptism. But Mother in her excited way was rampant.
> What! Would she permit any man to say aloud over the body of
> her pure and precious infant that he was born in sin and ask for
> sponsors? Never! That settled it and they named him Louis Henri
> Sullivan.

While Grandfather List may have been scornful of religion, his
passion for the order and splendor of the solar system made him
well aware of the mystery and wonder of creation, an awareness, we

can assume, he passed on to his grandson. Sullivan's description of a sunrise, although written some sixty years later, makes us feel how deeply he must have experienced it. While watching the sun disappear behind the hills one evening, his grandfather told him that a sunrise was even more overwhelming. The next morning

> ... he stood, gazing wistfully over the valley ... as the top of the
> sun emerging from behind the hills, its slow-revealing disc reaching
> full form, ascended, fiery, imperious and passionate, to confront
> him. Chilled and spellbound, he in turn became impassioned with
> splendor and awe, with wonder and he knew not what, as the
> great red orb, floating clear of the hilltops overwhelmed him. ...

With such intensely personal experiences to make him aware of the created world, he began to perceive that man has within himself the ability to plan and build, to create. The perception grew when the family spent a summer at Newburyport, his father taking him to see great, wooden ships being built; not long after he went across Massachusetts through the Berkshires with his grandfather by train, all of which brought home to him what man could do. Riding in the train, "Louis again felt the power of man. The thought struck deep, that what was bearing him along was solely the power of man; the living power to wish, to will, to do." This belief in man's power and his responsibility to use it "beneficently," as he later put it, became central to the development of Louis Sullivan's thought and is the subject of his book.

It was while he was still in school that he first became aware of buildings. Most Boston buildings depressed him; the State House, for instance, with its golden dome, "seemed to him a thin, stingy old woman." But one building had a particular appeal to him, "a Masonic Temple built of hewn granite, light grey in tone and joyous in aspect." The manner in which a twelve-year-old boy responded to this building offers startling evidence of the architectural genius that was to come: ". . . as he returned again and again to his wonder building, the single one that welcomed him, the solitary one that gave out a perfume of romance, that radiated joy, that seemed fresh and full of laughter."

It was under the powerful influence of such impressions that

Louis made up his mind to become an architect. While walking one day on Commonwealth Avenue in Boston, he happened to see a dignified, bearded gentleman, wearing top hat and frock coat, come out of an unfinished building and get into a carriage waiting at the curb. When he asked one of the workmen who this man was, and was told that he was the "archeetec" who designed the building, laid it out, and prescribed what the men who were building it were to do, and did it all "out of his head"—just as an architect had done for his beloved Masonic Temple—Louis' mind was made up: he would become an architect. When he broke the news to his father, the latter told him that he had it in mind for him to become a "scientific farmer," but if he wished to become an architect, he was prepared to provide the necessary education. It was agreed, then, "that Louis should remain in Boston to complete his General Education; after that to a Technical School; and, some day—Abroad." And so, as it happened, that was the way it worked out.

At the time it was decided that Louis should become an architect, his father took his mother to live in Chicago, on the assumption that it was imperative that she get away from the damp sea air of Boston. Louis was sent again to live with his grandparents, which meant going in and out of Boston every day by train and a walk of one mile at each end in all kinds of weather—"an accepted part of the day's doings, accepted without a murmur."

Schooling now had an objective, preparation for the study of architecture, and he applied himself "in gluttonous introspection, as one with a fixed idea, an unalterable purpose." He made up his mind to graduate with honors, and in June 1870 he received, as he says, "his first and last diploma." The following September, at the age of fourteen, he passed the examination and entered Boston English High School.

The experience of the English High School was a great awakening. On the first day his class of some forty boys was addressed by the "master" to whom they had been assigned, Moses Woolson. The address made a profound impression on him, so profound that he could recall it almost word for word more than fifty years later. The master's manner, he remembered, was like that of "a first mate taking on a fresh crew." He began:

Boys, you don't know me, but you soon will. The discipline here
will be rigid. You have come here to learn and I'll see that you
do. I will not only do my share but I will make you do yours.
You are here under my care; no other man shall interfere with
you. I rule here—I am master here—as you will soon discover.
You are here as wards in my charge; ... I accept the responsibility involved as a high, exacting duty I owe to myself and
equally to you. I will give to you all that I have; you shall give
me all that you have. But mark you: The first rule of discipline
shall be SILENCE.... The second rule shall be STRICT ATTEN-
TION: You are here to *learn*, to *think*, to *concentrate* on the
matter in hand, to hold your minds steady. The third rule shall
cover ALERTNESS. You shall be awake all the time—body and
brain; you shall cultivate promptness, speed, nimbleness, dexter-
ity of mind. The fourth rule: You shall learn to LISTEN; to *listen*
in *silence* with the *whole* mind, not part of it; ... for sound listening is a basis for sound thinking; sympathetic listening is a
basis for sympathetic, worth-while thinking; accurate listening is
a basis of accurate thinking. Finally you are to learn to OB-
SERVE, to REFLECT, to DISCRIMINATE. But this subject is of
such high importance, so much above your present understanding, that I will not comment upon it now; it is not to be ap-
proached without due preparation. I shall not start you with a
jerk, but tighten the lines bit by bit until I have you firmly in
hand at the most spirited pace you can go.

Boston English High School was an enormously stimulating
educational experience for Louis Sullivan and gave him a solid
basis for further intellectual development for which he craved. The
straightforward, no-nonsense statement with which the "master"
began the school year, as Louis said, "amazed, thunder-struck,
dumb-founded," but more than that it left him "over-joyed." In
Moses Woolson, he said, he had encountered "not alone a man
but a TEACHER. ..."
The studies on which he set the highest value were algebra,
geometry, English literature, botany, mineralogy and the French
language. All of them, he said were "revelations." "Algebra had

startled him; for, through its portal he entered an unsuspected world of symbols." "Geometry delighted him because of its nicety, its exactitude of relationships, its weird surprises. . . ." Botany taught him the "true story" of the "most secret intimacies and the organization" of the world of growing things. "Minerology was new and revealing, the common stones had begun as it were to talk to him in their own words." Of the French language, "he was ardent, for he had France in view." But it was for the teaching of English literature that he received the highest praise, for it opened for him

> . . . the great world of words, of ordered speech, the marvelous vehicle whereby were conveyed every human thought and feel-ing . . . ; and to his ever widening view, it soon arose before him as a vast treasure house wherein was stored, in huge accumulation, a record of the thoughts, the deeds, the hopes, the joys, the sorrows, and the triumphs of mankind.

After spending two years at the English High School he passed the entrance examination and was admitted to the School of Architecture at the Massachusetts Institute of Technology. He stayed at MIT for only one year. Even though he learned not only to "draw but to draw very well" and was introduced to the technical side of architecture, the overly academic approach to architecture with its emphasis on the "Five Orders of Architecture" did not appeal to him. He could "see no future there," and made up his mind to "see what architecture might be like in practice." With a grandfather and an uncle in Philadelphia who, he knew, would welcome him, he set off with the idea of finding a place in an architect's office, which he did in the firm of Furness and Hewitt. It was "his great good fortune to have made his entry into the practical world in an office where standards were so high—where talent was so manifestly taken for granted, and the atmosphere the free and easy one of a true work shop savoring of the guild where craftsmanship was paramount and personal." His apprenticeship in these pleasant and stimulating surroundings ended with the failure of the banking firm of Jay Cooke & Co. and the subsequent panic of 1873, when he set out for Chicago, knowing that he would be as welcomed there by his mother and father as he had been by his grandfather and uncle in Philadelphia.

On the day before Thanksgiving 1873 he arrived in Chicago, only two years after the devastating conflagration of 1871. The prairies of northern Indiana and the first sight of Lake Michigan over-whelmed him. The train, he said,

> plowed its way through miles of shanties, disheartening and dirty gray. It reached its terminal at an open shed. Louis tramped the platform, stopped, looked toward the city, ruins about him; looked at the sky; and as one alone, stamped his foot, raised his hand and cried in full voice: THIS IS THE PLACE FOR ME!

To be sure, the financial panic had reached Chicago, but with an entire city to rebuild Louis was able to find a place in the office of Major William Le Baron Jenney. He was attracted to his office because he had learned that it was there that the Portland Block had been designed, one of the few buildings he had seen since arriving in Chicago that, he thought, showed some evidence of "talent in design." The office of Major Jenney was without doubt the best possible introduction he could have found to the self-confident, virile, dynamic city where he was to live out his life and make his reputation. Jenney had studied in Paris, but in the Ecole Polytech-nique rather than the Beaux Arts, and had served as major of engineers in Sherman's army during the Civil War. "Louis soon found out that the Major was not, really, in his heart, an engineer at all, but by nature, and in toto a *bon vivant*, a gourmet." He was also an accomplished raconteur and "a master of the chafing dish," but for all that had designed the first iron-framed building and ran a thoroughly professional office.

On the stool next to his "sat patient Martin Roche," later of the firm Holabird and Roche, and the foreman was John Edelman, who soon became Louis' fast friend and teacher. "Never before or since," he wrote of him fifty years later, "has Louis met his equal in vitality, in verity, and in perspicacity of thought." It was Edelman who first introduced him to the music of Richard Wagner, at the Sunday afternoon concerts at the North Side Turner Hall, which made a profound impression on him:

Here, indeed, had been lifted a great veil, revealing anew, refreshing as dawn, the enormous power of man to build as a mirage, the fabric of his dreams, and with his wand of toil to make them real. Thus Louis's heart was stirred, his courage was tenfolded in this raw city by the Great Lake in the West.

But as much as he enjoyed and was stimulated by the winter and spring in Chicago, he still dreamed of the Ecole des Beaux Arts in Paris, the "fountainhead of theory," and on the tenth of July 1874 he sailed from New York for the next stage of his development.

After settling himself in Paris, Louis was startled to discover that the examination for entrance to the Beaux Arts were scheduled to begin in eight weeks and covered a range of subjects for which he was not prepared. But he was determined to make the grade and decided that by working eighteen hours a day, with a tutor in French and a class in mathematics, he could do it. He got on well with his fellow students, who admired his fluency in their language, but one day he was told, "We would have you know, friend, you are not properly dressed." Only the working classes, they explained, wore such a cap as his, and only sporting people such clothes and shoes. "You shall dress like a student," they told him, "and be one of us." As soon as it could be done, therefore, "Louis appeared in tall silk hat, an infant beard, long tail coat, and trousers of dark material, polished shoes, kid gloves, and jaunty cane. Louis felt self-conscious, but he was met with so voluble a chorus of approval that he changed his tune, studied carefully the student manual so as to be one of them. . . ." When the great day of examination, which were to be oral, written, and in drawing, lasting for three weeks, finally arrived, he felt that he was prepared.

The examination testing his proficiency in free-hand drawing and mechanical drawing, as well as in preparing a simple architectural project, presented no problem for him. Following the examination in mathematics the professor told him, "Monsieur Sullivan: you have the mathematical imagination . . ." The oral examinations in history are of particular interest, not only in themselves, but for what they tell us a student was expected to know. The examination was presided over by a professor and was public. Instead of questions about dates and specific events, as he had expected from his American experience, the first question seemed almost to take the ground out from under him: "Monsieur, will you be kind enough to tell me the story of the Hebrew People?" Having read fairly extensively in the Old Testament and having heard more, as he said, than he had read, he was able to give a good account of himself, encouraged as he went along by the comments and questions of the professor, who, at one point, asked him, "What impressed him most vividly in the story of the Jews?" To this he replied, "The emergence and vivid personality of Jehovah, their God."

The second question asked for an account of the ten Roman emperors. The third question began with these remarks by the professor:

"Monsieur, I see you have a certain faculty, a bit crude as yet, of making word pictures, of discerning something real beneath the glamour of the surface, which it is the particular business of the true historian to uncover. Now, therefore, as this is to be the last question, do your best and give me an intimate account of the times of Francis First."

Louis "did this with joy." Because it was the time of Leonardo da Vinci, he had studied the period with particular care and devotion. Then, after explaining the purpose of the examinations, which was "not to ascertain an array of facts. . .but to discern the degree of intelligence possessed by the candidate; . . ." the professor concluded: "I can now do no less for your gratification and as well as my own, than to give you the highest rating and to wish you happiness," whereupon Louis received the card of admission to the Ecole des Beaux Arts, which was good until the age of thirty. He, at this time, was eighteen, and had exactly three years of formal education behind him, two years at Boston English High School and one year at MIT.

He entered "heart and soul" into the work of the atelier where the formal architectural studies of the school were concentrated, enjoyed the comradeship of his fellow students, and took advantage of everything Paris had to offer—museums, monuments, exhibitions, gardens, "unforgettable midnight masses at Notre Dame"—but for all that, it didn't give him what he wanted.

> He familiarized himself thoroughly with the theory of the School, which, in his mind, settled down to a theory of *plan*, yielding results of extraordinary brilliancy, but which, after all, was not the reality he sought, but an abstraction, a method, a state of mind, that was local and specific; not universal. . . .there was for him a fatal residuum of artificiality, which gave him a secret sense of misery.

By the next spring he was on his way back to Chicago and his friend and teacher John Edelman.

The experience which without doubt made the most profound impression on Louis Sullivan during that winter in Europe was his three days in Rome, of which two were spent in the Sistine Chapel. While studying the history of architecture he had run into three small volumes of the philosophy of art by Hippolyte Taine, an author he had first come to know while under the tutelage of Moses Woolson. In one of these books Louis encountered the statement that Michelangelo's painting of the Last Judgment in the Sistine Chapel "was *obviously* done on *momentum*, as compared with the vigor of the ceiling." This remark "alarmed him" because, not willing to trust the judgment of such a subtle change in the work of a great artist to anyone else, he must see for himself. To his great relief, he found it self-evident. He now knew that "he could see anything that the eye could see."

During that brief visit to the Sistine Chapel he not only confirmed the keenness of his eye, but also, more than that, "felt and saw a great Free Spirit." All that he believed and thought about man's power, began when, as a small boy, he had watched strong men build a stone wall, then riding on a train through the Berkshires, seemed to have been confirmed in the Sistine Chapel:

> Here was the living presence of a man who had *done things in the beneficence of power.* . . . And in this great outpouring which encompassed him, he saw the Dreamer at his work. For no hand, unaided, could do this; no intellect unaided could do this; Imagination alone could do this; and Imagination, *looked into,* revealed

itself as uncompromising faith in Life, as faith in man, and especial faith in his wondrous powers. He saw that Imagination passes beyond reason and is a consummated act of Instinct—the primal power of Life at work.

His response to the great work of Michelangelo, written no doubt not as experienced by an eighteen-year-old boy, but from the background of fifty years of life, contains the guiding principle of Louis Sullivan's life and work.

Settling Down
to Work

WHEN LOUIS CAME BACK TO CHICAGO from Paris in the spring of 1875, jobs in architects' offices were scarce—the Panic of 1873 had still not spent itself. He used the opportunity to explore the city, making "his twenty miles or more in the course of a systematic reconnaissance on foot. When this adventure had come to its end, he knew every nook and corner of the city and its environs . . ." He was soon able to pick up small jobs in various architects' offices, and by his skill and speed as a draftsman began to get more substantial assignments. He used his spare time to study such engineering manuals as were available. Two great projects at the time which especially attracted his interest and admiration were the triple-arch Eads Bridge across the Mississippi at St. Louis and the cantilever bridge across the chasm of the Kentucky River. He was so impressed by the daring of such projects—both examples of "man in his power to create beneficently"—that he seriously thought about becoming an engineer, but conditions improved: "His engagements in offices grew longer, he began to prosper. The quality of his work was improving. He had passed the day of his majority, and was now looking out for himself. . . . He was a man now, and he knew it."

It was at this time that Louis's friend and mentor, John Edelman, reappeared in the city, having spent a "dull spell" trying his hand as a farmer in Iowa. One winter day he showed up at the restaurant where a congenial group of young architects and draftsmen, including Louis, made a practice of having lunch together. Edelman soon joined the group and "as usual," Louis said, ". . . monopolized the conversation, unless rudely interrupted." Having in the meantime become a member of the firm of Burling and Adler, Edelman one day suggested after lunch that Louis come with him to meet Dankmar Adler. Except for a favorable impression on both sides, nothing came of the meeting. Louis was satisfied with things as they were—"his days were for work; his nights for study. . . ." Then, early in 1879, Edelman asked Louis to come to see him in the evening, he had something to say to him, namely that Adler had "cut loose" from Burling and needed just such talent as Louis could bring into his firm. Following the second call on Adler, it was agreed that Louis was to take charge of Adler's office and have a free hand. Then, if all went well, and if they should get along, there would be "something tangible in the background." This Louis quickly realized was his first great opportunity, and he lost no time in taking advantage of it.

Soon three substantial projects came into the firm, an office building, known as the Borden Block, a theater, and a large residence. Adler gave his future partner, who was only twenty-four at the time, every opportunity to go ahead on his own and was particularly helpful in "matters of building technique of which he had a complete grasp. . . ." They became warm friends, and on the first day of May 1881 the name of the firm Adler & Sullivan appeared on the front door of the aforementioned Borden Block. Thus began the most productive period of Sullivan's life and an association that was to continue until 1895 and have a profound and lasting effect on the practice of architecture.

In describing his state of mind at the beginning of his partnership with Dankmar Adler, Sullivan speaks of his determination to "make an architecture that fitted its functions." It was to be an architecture in which "all practical demands of utility should be paramount," which meant that "he would put to the test a formula he had evolved, through long contemplation of living things,

namely that *form follows function . . .*" Because he often repeated
this formulation and obviously attached great importance to it the
question can be justly asked, What did he really mean by it? Would
the contemporary steel and glass office building be an example of
form following function? Such a building, from one point of view,
admirably fulfills its function of providing office space in the most
efficient possible way, but it is certainly no source of inspiration
either to those who work in it, in its cold, stark efficiency, nor to
those who must look at it. If the function of a building is to provide
four walls and a roof, then the glass and steel building is functional,
but if architecture is an art, as Sullivan firmly believed, and if the
function of art is to raise the vision of man to higher things, then
the glass and steel building is not functional; it is a blight on the
landscape, an affront to the created world, and a denial of man's
humanity.

Louis Sullivan was convinced that architecture is a reflection of
the circumstances, character and aspiration of its time. In one of his
*Kindergarten Chats,** he says: "Nothing more clearly reflects the
status and tendencies of a people than its buildings. They are the
emanation of a people; they visualize for us the soul of our people."
The medieval cathedral, if Sullivan is correct, can be assumed to be
the expression of the age of faith, just as Chicago's Sears Tower—
the "world's tallest building"—is an expression of the age of the
computer, the jet airplane, and atomic fission.

It is interesting to note that the *Kindergarten Chats,* according to
its publisher, was first printed in 1901 in fifty-two successive numbers of *The Interstate Architect and Builders,* described, again by
the publisher, as "a weekly trade journal, now long defunct, of
limited circulation and of negligible importance. Nevertheless," he
goes on to say, "it reached most of the architects of the middle west
and thus found its way into draughting rooms where were the very
ones for whom the *Chats* were written—to whom, indeed, they

---

* *Kindergarten Chats on Architecture, Education, and Democracy,* edited and introduced by Claude F. Bragdon (Lawrence, Kansas Scarab Fraternity Press,
1934).

were addressed—young men serving their apprenticeship to the profession of architecture."

One of the two epigrams in *Kindergarten Chats* comes from William Wordsworth's *The River Duddon, After-Thought*. Wordsworth's view of Form and Function echoes Sullivan's concept of "Form Follows Function":

> *Still glides the stream and shall forever glide;*
> *The form remains, the Function never dies;*
> *While we the brave, the mighty, and the wise,*
> *We men, who in our morn of youth defied*
> *The elements, must vanish;— be it so!*
> *Enough, if something from our hands have power*
> *To live, and act, and serve the future hour*
> *And if, as toward the silent land we go,*
> *Through love, through hope, and faith's transcendent dower,*
> *We feel that we are greater than we know.*

The firm of Adler & Sullivan prospered. It was a good combination—Adler, some twelve years older than Sullivan, was much respected as a man of integrity and for his competence as an engineer, while Sullivan, for his part, was already gaining a reputation for imaginative design. Several commercial projects gave Sullivan the opportunity to apply his theory of the relation of form to function, particularly in providing a maximum of daylight, which led to the use of slender piers, a combination of masonry and iron, and "the beginnings of the vertical system." The first large project of the firm was the Auditorium Building in Chicago, completed in 1889, and still, as Roosevelt University, a monument to Adler & Sullivan. The building originally included an auditorium seating 4,250, renowned for its remarkable acoustics, a hotel, an office building, and a tower. The labor of designing and completing this enormous project, which required four years, left Sullivan completely spent, and he said, doubtlessly shortened Adler's life.

The Auditorium Building was of masonry construction and came when steel-frame construction was just beginning, a development in which Chicago architects were taking the lead. "The architects of Chicago welcomed the steel-frame and did something with it. The

architects of the East were appalled by it and could make no contribution to it." So remarks Louis Sullivan and then goes on to say:

> In and by itself, considered *solus* so to speak, the lofty steel frame
> makes a powerful appeal to the architectural imagination where
> there is any. Where imagination is absent and its place usurped by
> timid pedantry the case is hopeless. The appeal and the inspiration
> lie, of course, in the element of loftiness, in the suggestion of slen-
> derness and aspiration, the soaring quality as of a thing rising from
> the earth as a unitary utterance. . . .

Sullivan mistakenly gives Holabird and Roche credit for designing the first steel frame building, the Tacoma Building in Chicago,
but having said that, adds the categorical statement that steel frame
construction "was given first authentic recognition and expression
in the exterior treatment of the Wainright Building, a nine-story
office structure, by Louis Sullivan's own hand." The Wainright
Building was designed to be what it was, a tall building; it did not
pretend to look like something else—a Gothic Cathedral, for example, or a Roman temple with layers of floors added on top of the
columns. Frank Lloyd Wright, who was working as a draftsman at
the time, described the dramatic moment when Sullivan showed
him his first sketch of the building: "I was perfectly aware of what
had happened. This was the great Louis Sullivan moment. The
skyscraper as a new thing beneath the sun . . . with virtue, individu-
ality, beauty all its own, as the tall building was born." He goes on
to say that it was Sullivan who "first perceived the tall building as a
harmonious unit—its height triumphant."* It is altogether appropriate to Sullivan's genius that his concept, both literally and figu-
ratively, fulfilled his definition of architecture as Art that would, as
he insisted it should, uplift the eyes of the world.

---

* Quoted in Willard Connely, *Louis Sullivan* (New York, 1960) p. 130—131.

The Collapse
of a Career

THE *Autobiography of an Idea* ends with the Chicago World's Fair of 1893, as Louis Sullivan's architectural career, in substance, did also. His only large project after the Fair was what is now the Carson, Pirie, Scott department store in Chicago, with its characteristic clean lines, large windows, and beautiful "Sullivanesque" floral decorations. After 1900 his only commissions were eight banks in small, midwestern towns, now much admired as masterpieces of design. His great years as an architect were behind him.

The World's Columbian Exposition is still remembered as Chicago's great triumph. There was the "Court of Honor," its dramatic centerpiece, presided over by a monumental gilded statue at the end of a lagoon flanked by a spectacular array of white buildings in classical style; there were exhibits of art, machinery, locomotives, dynamos; native villages, Egyptian dancers. With all this, plus lagoons, wooded islands and Lake Michigan as a background, even such a worldly figure as Henry Adams was bedazzled, along with hundreds of thousands of others from all parts of the country. For Louis Sullivan, who regarded the Fair as "a test of American culture," it was an unmitigated disaster.

When the ten architects selected by Daniel Burnham, who had been named chief of construction—five from the East and five from the West—met in February 1891 to examine the site and work out preliminary plans and procedures, each architect was assigned a building. Sullivan came out with the Transportation Building, and because he had no intention of making it conform to the white, neoclassic buildings that were to adorn the Court of Honor—which his biographer says he described, in a rather heated discussion, as "a parade of white elephants"—had to be content with a site off to one side. All of this made it clear to him that rather than a "symbol," as he had hoped, "of the city's basic significance as offspring of the prairie, the lake and the portage. But 'hustle' was the word. Make it big, make it stunning, knock 'em down."

> The damage wrought by the World's Fair will last for half a century from its date, if not longer. It has penetrated deep into the constitution of the American mind, . . . Thus we have now the abounding freedom of Eclecticism, the winning smile of taste, but no architecture. For Architecture, be it known, is dead.

In spite of the collapse of Sullivan's career as an architect, he would write at the end of his book, and nearing the end of his life:

> . . . here Louis underwent that morphosis which is all there is of him, that spiritual illumination which knows no why and no wherefore, no hither and no hence, that peace which is life's sublimation, timeless and spaceless. Yet he never lost his footing on the earth; never came the sense of immortality: One life surely is enough if lived and fulfilled: That we have yet to learn the true significance of man; to realize the destruction we have wrought; to come to a consciousness of our moral instability; For man is godlike enough did he but know it—did he but choose, did he but remove his wrappings and his blinders, and say good-bye to his superstitions and his fear.

The reader of Louis H. Sullivan's *Autobiography of an Idea* will encounter a strong-willed man of unimpeachable integrity, a man who developed his remarkable gifts to their utmost and employed them, to use one of his favorite words, beneficently.

Afterthoughts . . .
Some Reminiscences and a Hope

THE REMARKABLE ERA of creative achievement that began following the Great Fire of 1871 and reached a climax with the World's Fair of 1893, as has been seen, had run its course by the turn of the century. In less than thirty years, Chicago had not only found the energy and resources to rebuild from the vast destruction of the Fire, but to found its major cultural institutions: the Public Library, the Art Institute, the Chicago Symphony Orchestra, the Newberry and Crerar Libraries, the University of Chicago, and the Field Museum. By the end of the decade of the Fair, with a population approaching two million, having become the railroad center of the country and a major manufacturing and distribution center, Chicago had truly become a great city. Further, the creative ferment inspired by the Fair had attracted a number of artists and authors to the city, leading to the establishment of three publishing firms and an innovative, lively literary journal, *The Chap-Book*, which with *The Dial*, meant that Chicago had two nationally recognized literary journals of high quality. All of this led to the expectation, as Hamlin Garland later put it, that "Chicago was about to take its place among the literary capitals of the world."

The success of the Fair was followed by severe, grinding depression, with much unemployment, social unrest and violent strikes. The impressive buildings of the Fair's "White City," their facades largely built of lath and plaster, began to deteriorate and they became havens, until eventually destroyed by fire, for jobless, homeless men. The last of the three publishing firms, launched with such hope and confidence, brought out its final book in 1905. *The Chap-Book* had gone under during the war with Spain. Chicago, in Garland's words, "fell back into something like its former drabness of business enterprise." The Chicago of the new century, the Chicago that had inspired and provided the setting for Dreiser's *Sister Carrie*, was a hard, driving, commercial city. In such a city the idealism that had moved Herbert Stone and Hannibal Ingalls Kimball to found a publishing firm and an innovative literary magazine evoked little understanding or support.

It is instructive to compare the hopes of those who took a leading part in the founding of the cultural institutions of Chicago with what has become of them and of the city of which they are a part. The Art Institute is truly internationally known, the Chicago Symphony equally recognized and honored, and the University of Chicago is justly respected as a center of higher learning and research, but Chicago has by no means become one of the literary capitals of the world. If the contemporary *Chicago Magazine*, which has taken the place once occupied by *The Dial* and *The Chap-Book*, is indicative of the literary standards of contemporary Chicago, one can hardly say that much progress has been made, despite the far greater proportion of Chicagoans who are now given an opportunity for education, from high school through the university. Rather than literature, the chief subjects of interest of *Chicago Magazine* seems to be restaurants, fashions, shopping and travel, all of which, it must be assumed, is what its readers want. Unfortunately, Chicago can make no claim either to a distinguished, general publishing firm, which Hamlin Garland considered the other requirement, besides a literary magazine of recognized quality, for a city to claim the stature of literary center.

Why, it seems appropriate to ask again, has Chicago never been able to support a substantial general publishing house? There have been numerous attempts to publish serious books in Chicago, as we have seen, but those who have achieved some degree of success have usually moved to the East, while others have fallen by the wayside. Chicago, it seems, does not offer a hospitable climate to a book publisher. The literary agents are nearly all in New York, as are the bookclubs and the influential magazines and newspapers that review books; in short, the apparatus on which the publisher depends. There may also be a less obvious reason—book publishing is apparently not "the thing to do." A Chicago book publisher will frequently be asked, as I know from personal experience, "What does a publisher do?" as though he doesn't really belong in Chicago, and he finally may well come to the conclusion that he doesn't.

In spite of the remarkable success of Stone & Kimball and their successor, Herbert Stone & Co., the national recognition they won and the place they made for themselves in Chicago with their literary teas, readings and other similar gatherings, one has the impression, as we have seen, that Stone's parents had misgivings about their son's activities which were not entirely based on concern about the financial situation of the firm, although this undoubtedly played a part. It was the senior Stone, whether intentionally or not, who broke up the partnership which resulted in Kimball buying the assets of the firm and taking it to New York. There he did some successful publishing but for lack of capital soon went bankrupt, after which Herbert Stone brought the firm back to Chicago. With adequate capital and proper management, both well within the capability of the Stone family to provide, it seems possible that Stone & Kimball could have become an eminently successful publishing firm, and in so doing been a great boon to the cultural life of Chicago.

But Chicago, it must be conceded, is primarily a commercial city, which is doubtless the reason that it has never shown much interest in such esoteric activities as literary magazines or book publishing. Henry Fuller, who must have known Chicago society as well as anyone, has one of the characters in his novel, *With the Procession*, remark, "Chicago is the only great city in the world in which all its citizens have come for the one common, avowed object of making money." In this respect I have never forgotten the comment of my father, a businessman himself, who always encouraged and supported my publishing career, but knowing Chicago as he did, once cautioned me, "If you ever start making money in that business you are going into, you'll probably be publishing the wrong sort of books."

· During the early days of my publishing firm when I was bringing out some significant books, some of which were successful, but still trying desperately to put the firm on a solid basis, I became acquainted with a man who, as I think about him and the many conversations I had with him, seems to me, if in a rather extreme way, to be representative of Chicago. He was of the generation of my father. He was brought to the city, he once told me, as a boy from Rhode Island by his father, and he took great pride in the fact that he came from one of the very early American families. When he got into some sort of scrape while in school, his father told him, as he related the story to me, "If that's the way you feel about it, you had better get to work." His father found him a job in an investment house on LaSalle Street, of which he eventually became sole owner and made into one of the largest bond-underwriting firms in the country. He was unmarried and lived with his two unmarried sisters at the best address in Chicago.

My original purpose in going to see him was to ask him to invest some money in my firm, money which I very much needed. His reply was always the same, "I would like to, but my money is all tied up in my business." He did, however, invite me to have lunch with him from time to time. He seemed to enjoy my accounts of the vagaries of the publishing business, and seemed particularly to enjoy it when I invited him to meet a visiting author, William F. Buckley, Jr., Westbrook Pegler, or William Henry Chamberlin, for example. The South African poet, Roy Campbell, who was a delightful companion and a wonderful storyteller, made a great impression on my investment banker friend, who remarked after a lunch I had arranged for a small group, "If you have spent your life grubbing for money, it is a wonderful experience to meet such a man." For his part, on the rare occasions Roy might have had a little money in his pocket, he was as likely as not to give it to the first person he ran into who appeared to need it more than he did.

My father told me that if I expected to get any money out of my banker friend, I was wasting my time, which I soon discovered to be true, but I enjoyed his company and the stories he told me about his experiences with such Chicago figures as Samuel Insull and J. Ogden Armour, for whom he had acted as investment banker. I particularly remember his account of a trip to Poland some time in the 'twenties, when the Polish government had invited him over, hoping to induce him to float a loan. After describing the royal treatment he had been given, he went on to say that he decided that Poland was a "comic opera" country, and declined to handle their bond issue. When he arrived back in New York, there was a message from Andrew Mellon, who was then Secretary of the Treasury, asking him to stop in Washington on his return to Chicago. Mellon, he said, questioned him closely about Poland, and upon hearing his conclusion that it was a "comic opera" country, called his Pittsburgh office and told them, "Sell the Polish bonds." He told me many such stories, including how he had handled a bond issue for the German industrialist, Hugo Stinnes, thus rescuing Stinnes from being driven into a corner, as he put it, by a group of New York bankers, or how he acquired, and then sold, the *Cincinnati Enquirer*—all, of course, with great profit to himself. One day, when we were having lunch in the Chicago Club, former governor Adlai Stevenson stopped by to speak to him. After Stevenson had left, my banker friend remarked, "He was my lawyer at one time." When I asked if he was a good lawyer, my friend considered for a moment—he was not one to make hasty judgments—and said, "The answer is no."

We were walking from his office to his club one day in August. It was a typical Chicago day for that time of year, with a southwest, hot, dry wind and with much dirt and dust in the air. "Isn't Chicago a dirty city," I remarked, at which point he stopped dead in his tracks, looked me full in the face, and replied, quite emphatically, "But it's a good place to make money." Making money, I think, was his only real interest, and able, energetic and single-minded as he was, he made lots of it. He was a striking-looking man, broad-shouldered, erect. With the manner of a dignified, successful banker, he was a well known figure as he walked from his home on Lake Shore Drive to his office on LaSalle Street, as he did for many years. He lived comfortably, but not extravagantly. He made money, not for what he wished to do with it, but because he enjoyed the game of making it, of matching his wits and skills against the New York bankers with whom he competed. That he had no particular objective in accumulating money is demonstrated by the fact that, besides a comfortable fortune to each of his two sisters, he left his entire estate to the trust department of a Chicago bank with instructions to give it away within five years to organizations enjoying tax exemption.

There were, of course, influential people in Chicago who had other interests than making money, as such institutions as the libraries, the Symphony, the Art Institute and the University of Chicago testify. An example of the other Chicago is Charles L. Hutchinson, who can serve as a counterpart to my investment banker friend. His father came from Lynn, Massachusetts and arrived in Chicago in 1858 when his son Charles was four. The older Hutchinson became one of the great grain traders of his time—he is reputed to have made a million dollars in a single day when he cornered the wheat market—and was the founder of a leading bank, the Corn Exchange, of which his son, rather reluctantly it would seem, eventually became president. As was the case with Henry Fuller, the father was determined that his son should go into business, with similar results. Having no interest in trading or speculation, Charles Hutchinson used his inherited wealth to support the many cultural institutions in which he took an active part. He became president of the Art Institute when it was founded in 1882 out of the Chicago Academy of Design, and remained president, taking a leading role in its management, until his death in 1924.

The Art Institute was by no means Hutchinson's only interest. It was Charles Hutchinson, as president of the Commercial Club, who brought the newly founded University of Chicago to the attention of its members and was therefore instrumental in raising the $400,000 John D. Rockefeller had required to secure his gift. Hutchinson became the first treasurer of the University and with his friend Martin Ryerson, the first president of the board, was one of the most active trustees in the early days of the university. The Commercial Club, it is worth mentioning, was a constructive influence in the cultural life of the city. It was the Commercial Club that underwrote and promoted Burnham's Chicago Plan, and it was at a meeting of the Club that the plan for the Auditorium was proposed and supported, as was the present building of the Art Institute.

It was a rather small group who took the decisive part in the founding of the leading cultural institutions of the city. Among the names which seem to appear most often, although by no means exclusively, besides Charles Hutchinson and Martin Ryerson, are Edward E. Ayer, Watson F. Blair, Nathaniel K. Fairbank, Harold N. Higginbotham, Albert A. Sprague, Franklin Macveigh. They all knew each other, belonged to the same clubs, came from similar backgrounds, shared the same standards, and had a sense of responsibility for the city to which they owed their success. In their civic responsibility, their awareness of the needs of the community, and the coherence of their objectives, the cultural leaders of Chicago in those days constituted an elite, and without a responsible elite such creative achievement would have been impossible.

One wonders if such a group, with like interests and resources, will ever again come to dominate the cultural life of the city. It can, of course, be upsetting to speculate on the future. There are those, for instance, who insist that the electronics revolution, already altering through television the dispensing of news and entertainment and through computers the processing of information, will eventually eliminate altogether printed matter as we have known it, thus putting the book publisher in about the same category of relevance as the buggy whip manufacturer. On the other hand, in the fullness of time, through further education and refinement of taste, perhaps a demand will be created for the publication in traditional form of truly literate magazines and books. There may be another burst of creativity—after all, it has happened before, more than once as we have seen, and who is to say it might not happen again? After the Second World War a book entitled *Chicago's Left Bank* offered some hope, citing the work of writers like James T. Farrell, Meyer Levin, Willard Motley, Gwendolyn Brooks, the poetess who won a Pulitzer prize, and Saul Bellow, who went on to be awarded the Nobel prize in literature in 1976. Noteworthy, too, and to the credit of the city's intellectual and cultural leadership, its University can count some forty-five Nobel laureates among those who have been associated with it.

More recently, the city has become adorned with major public works of art, beginning with Pablo Picasso's looming, enigmatic sculpture in front of the City Hall, Alexander Calder's stabile before the Federal Center, Marc Chagall's *Four Seasons* mosaic mural at the First National Bank Plaza and Henry Moore's haunting skull-like sculpture, *Nuclear Energy*, on the University of Chicago campus, where the atomic age began. Further, there seems lately some diminution of the economic powers that have long dominated

Chicago; Sears, despite erecting the world's tallest building in downtown Chicago, lost its place as the nation's leading retailer; Marshall Field's, the city's pride in the taste and style of the goods presented, ran out of presidents who had made their long way to leadership from humble office boys and was taken over by a British conglomerate, then sold to a Minneapolis chain; the city's powerful banks have come upon hard times; and even such giants as International Harvester have been diminished by changing times and circumstances.

Still, anyone who regards New York closely these days can be forgiven the suspicion that it has become an impossible city, past its prime, if not definitely in decline. At the same time, a similar look at Chicago can lead to the notion that its New England heritage, firmly set by its founders, the persistent Protestant work ethic ever stronger than the cultural overtones, after so many generations, is fading at last. Perhaps Chicago is undergoing some significant alteration in the interplay between commercial and artistic impulses in the drive that carries its citizens forward; Caliban a bit subdued, it may well be. If that is true, then Chicago, a city that has taken the lead in many fields, might of a sudden see a true flowering of talent, a greater gathering of creative writers and imaginative publishers, and become at last a true literary center.

While that possibility might seem only a stubborn hope, the free spirit, rowdy sense of humor, and no-nonsense values of Chicagoans should not be underestimated. They have a down-to-earth way of seeing the world. At bottom, they know the ultimate worth and meaning of this life. Carl Sandburg appreciated this and liked to repeat the story* of the two ditchdiggers pondering the demise of the first Marshall Field, a dry goods salesman who had run up a fortune rumored to be $150 million. One workman, leaning on his shovel, asked, "How much did he leave?" and the other replied, "All of it."

---

* In *Slabs of the Sunburnt West*, Carl Sandburg, Harcourt Brace & Company, New York, 1922.

Index

Index

Index

Index